my **revisi⬤n** notes

Cambridge National Level 1/2

SPORT STUDIES

Symond Burrows
Sue Young

HODDER EDUCATION
AN HACHETTE UK COMPANY

Picture credits

Page 8 © Michael Spring/stock.adobe.com; page 10 © Entertainment Pictures/Alamy Stock Photo; page 12 © Microgen/stock.adobe.com; page 16 © Africa Studio/stock.adobe.com; page 18 © Seventyfour/stock.adobe.com; page 21 © Kaspars Grinvalds/stock.adobe.com; page 27 © Nenetus/stock.adobe.com; page 29 top © Leonard Zhukovsky/123 RF, bottom © / TM 2019 International Olympic Committee ("IOC") - All rights reserved.; page 32 © Boonchok/stock.adobe.com; page 38 © RedCap/Shutterstock.com; page 39 © Brambatti - Peri/EPA/Shutterstock; page 44 © British Cycling; page 51 © Microgen/stock.adobe.com; page 53 © WavebreakMediaMicro/stock.adobe.com; page 56 © Juice Images/Getty Images; page 62 © Andrii Kobryn/stock.adobe.com

Every effort has been made to trace all copyright holders, but if any have been inadvertently overlooked, the Publishers will be pleased to make the necessary arrangements at the first opportunity.

Although every effort has been made to ensure that website addresses are correct at time of going to press, Hodder Education cannot be held responsible for the content of any website mentioned in this book. It is sometimes possible to find a relocated web page by typing in the address of the home page for a website in the URL window of your browser.

Hachette UK's policy is to use papers that are natural, renewable and recyclable products and made from wood grown in well-managed forests and other controlled sources. The logging and manufacturing processes are expected to conform to the environmental regulations of the country of origin.

Orders: please contact Bookpoint Ltd, 130 Park Drive, Milton Park, Abingdon, Oxon OX14 4SE. Telephone: +44 (0)1235 827827. Fax: +44 (0)1235 400401. Email education@bookpoint. co.uk Lines are open from 9 a.m. to 5 p.m., Monday to Saturday, with a 24-hour message answering service. You can also order through our website: www.hoddereducation.co.uk

ISBN: 9781510478589

© Symond Burrows and Sue Young 2020

First published in 2020 by

Hodder Education,
An Hachette UK Company
Carmelite House
50 Victoria Embankment
London EC4Y 0DZ

www.hoddereducation.co.uk

Impression number 10 9 8 7 6 5 4 3 2 1
Year 2024 2023 2022 2021 2020

Cover photo © Africa Studio – stock.adobe.com

Typeset in India by Integra Software Services Ltd.

Printed in Spain.

A catalogue record for this title is available from the British Library.

Get the most from this book

Everyone has to decide his or her own revision strategy, but it is essential to review your work, learn it and test your understanding. These Revision Notes will help you to do that in a planned way, topic by topic. Use this book as the cornerstone of your revision and don't hesitate to write in it: personalise your notes and check your progress by ticking off each section as you revise.

Tick to track your progress

Use the revision planner on pages 4 and 5 to plan your revision, topic by topic. Tick each box when you have:

● revised and understood a topic

● tested yourself

● practised exam questions.

You can also keep track of your revision by ticking off each topic heading in the book. You may find it helpful to add your own notes as you work through each topic.

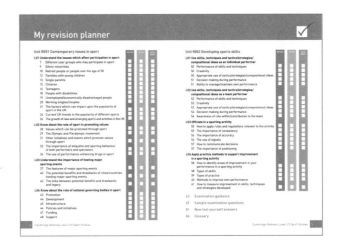

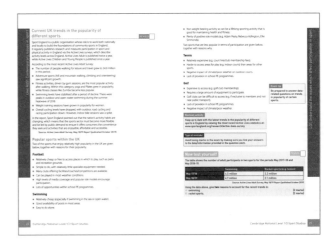

Features to help you succeed

Exam tips

Expert tips are given throughout the book to help you polish your exam technique in order to maximise your chances in the exam.

Typical mistakes

The authors identify the common mistakes candidates make and explain how you can avoid them.

Now test yourself

These short, knowledge-based questions provide the first step in testing your learning. Answers are given at the back of the book.

Revision activities

These activities will help you understand each topic in an interactive way.

Definitions and key words

Clear, concise definitions of essential key terms are provided.

My revision planner

Unit R051 Contemporary issues in sport

		REVISED	TESTED	EXAM READY

LO1 Understand the issues which affect participation in sport

7	Different user groups who may participate in sport	☐	☐	☐
9	Ethnic minorities	☐	☐	☐
10	Retired people or people over the age of 50	☐	☐	☐
12	Families with young children	☐	☐	☐
13	Single parents	☐	☐	☐
15	Children	☐	☐	☐
16	Teenagers	☐	☐	☐
18	People with disabilities	☐	☐	☐
19	Unemployed/economically disadvantaged people	☐	☐	☐
20	Working singles/couples	☐	☐	☐
21	The factors which can impact upon the popularity of sport in the UK	☐	☐	☐
24	Current UK trends in the popularity of different sports	☐	☐	☐
26	The growth of new and emerging sports and activities in the UK	☐	☐	☐

LO2 Know about the role of sport in promoting values

28	Values which can be promoted through sport	☐	☐	☐
29	The Olympic and Paralympic movement	☐	☐	☐
31	Other initiatives and events which promote values through sport	☐	☐	☐
32	The importance of etiquette and sporting behaviour of both performers and spectators	☐	☐	☐
34	The use of performance-enhancing drugs in sport	☐	☐	☐

LO3 Understand the importance of hosting major sporting events

37	The features of major sporting events	☐	☐	☐
40	The potential benefits and drawbacks of cities/countries hosting major sporting events	☐	☐	☐
42	The links between potential benefits and drawbacks and legacy	☐	☐	☐

LO4 Know about the role of national governing bodies in sport

43	Promotion	☐	☐	☐
44	Development	☐	☐	☐
45	Infrastructure	☐	☐	☐
46	Policies and initiatives	☐	☐	☐
47	Funding	☐	☐	☐
48	Support	☐	☐	☐

Unit R052 Developing sports skills

LO1 Use skills, techniques and tactics/strategies/compositional ideas as an individual performer

	REVISED	TESTED	EXAM READY
50 Performance of skills and techniques	☐	☐	☐
50 Creativity	☐	☐	☐
50 Appropriate use of tactics/strategies/compositional ideas	☐	☐	☐
51 Decision making during performance	☐	☐	☐
51 Ability to manage/maintain own performance	☐	☐	☐

LO2 Use skills, techniques and tactics/strategies/compositional ideas as a team performer

	REVISED	TESTED	EXAM READY
52 Performance of skills and techniques	☐	☐	☐
53 Creativity	☐	☐	☐
53 Appropriate use of tactics/strategies/compositional ideas	☐	☐	☐
54 Decision making during performance	☐	☐	☐
54 Awareness of role within/contribution to the team	☐	☐	☐

LO3 Officiate in a sporting activity

	REVISED	TESTED	EXAM READY
55 How to apply rules and regulations relevant to the activity	☐	☐	☐
55 The importance of consistency	☐	☐	☐
56 The importance of accuracy	☐	☐	☐
56 The use of signals	☐	☐	☐
57 How to communicate decisions	☐	☐	☐
57 The importance of positioning	☐	☐	☐

LO4 Apply practice methods to support improvement in a sporting activity

	REVISED	TESTED	EXAM READY
58 How to identify areas of improvement in your performance in a sporting activity	☐	☐	☐
58 Types of skills	☐	☐	☐
59 Types of practice	☐	☐	☐
60 Methods to improve own performance	☐	☐	☐
61 How to measure improvement in skills, techniques and strategies developed	☐	☐	☐

63 **Examination guidance**

67 **Sample examination questions**

81 **Now test yourself answers**

86 **Glossary**

Countdown to my exam

6–8 weeks to go

- Start by looking at the specification — make sure you know exactly what material you need to revise and the style of the examination.
- Use the revision planner on pages 4 and 5 to familiarise yourself with the topics. Organise your notes, making sure you have covered everything on the specification. The revision planner will help you to group your notes into topics.
- Work out a realistic revision plan that will allow you time for relaxation. Set aside days and times for all the subjects that you need to study, and stick to your timetable.
- Set yourself sensible targets. Break your revision down into focused sessions of around 40 minutes, divided by breaks. These Revision Notes organise the basic facts into short, memorable sections to make revising easier.

REVISED ☐

2–6 weeks to go

- Read through the relevant sections of this book and refer to the exam tips, typical mistakes and key terms. Tick off the topics as you feel confident about them. Highlight those topics you find difficult and look at them again in detail.
- Test your understanding of each topic by working through the 'Now test yourself' questions in the book. Look up the answers at the back of the book.
- Make a note of any problem areas as you revise, and ask your teacher to go over these in class.
- Look at past papers. They are one of the best ways to revise and practise your exam skills.
- Use the revision activities to try out different revision methods. For example, you can make notes using mind maps, spider diagrams or flash cards.
- Track your progress using the revision planner and give yourself a reward when you have achieved your target.

REVISED ☐

One week to go

- Try to fit in at least one more timed practice of an entire past paper and seek feedback from your teacher, comparing your work closely with the mark scheme.
- Check the revision planner to make sure you haven't missed out any topics. Brush up on any areas of difficulty by talking them over with a friend or getting help from your teacher.
- Attend any revision classes put on by your teacher. Remember, he or she is an expert at preparing people for examinations.

REVISED ☐

The day before the examination

- Flick through these Revision Notes for useful reminders, for example the exam tips, typical mistakes and key terms.
- Check the time and place of your examination.
- Make sure you have everything you need — extra pens and pencils, tissues, a watch, bottled water, sweets.
- Allow some time to relax and have an early night to ensure you are fresh and alert for the examination.

REVISED ☐

My exam

Date:...

Time: ....

Location: ....

Unit R051 Contemporary issues in sport

LO1 Understand the issues which affect participation in sport

Different user groups who may participate in sport

REVISED ☐

It is important that you can identify a range of different **user groups** who may participate in sport, before considering the possible barriers affecting the participation levels of each group, and the solutions to these barriers.

Table 1.1 describes the different user groups referred to in the specification – you must understand what is meant by each.

Table 1.1 User groups who participate in sport

User group	Explanation
Ethnic minorities (also known as BAME – Black, Asian and Minority Ethnic)	People not from the majority ethnic group in a country or within a community that is of a different nationality, culture or religion from the main group in that area or country
Retired people/people over 50	People over the age of 50, including elderly people, many of whom do not/no longer work
Families with young children	Parents or carers who look after children that may not be old enough to attend school
Single parents	Parents who are raising children without a partner
Children	Individuals up to the age of 12
Teenagers	Individuals aged 13–19
People with disabilities	Individuals with a physical or mental condition that affects or limits their senses, movements or ability to do certain activities
Unemployed/**economically disadvantaged** people	Individuals who do not have a paid job and/or have a low-income level
Working singles and couples	Working adults who may or may not have a partner

User group: A group of people with the same interests who use a particular service (e.g. a fitness class at a sports centre).

Economically disadvantaged: Someone who does not have enough income to meet basic needs and qualifies for state-organised benefits.

Figure 1.1 **Young man playing table tennis**

Exam tip

Make sure you know and can list different user groups who may participate in sport. You will need to apply your knowledge of these groups in a relevant way to scenarios or examples that may be given in an exam question.

Revision activity

Write down and learn the nine different user groups referred to. Memorise them so that you can pick the most appropriate one from the list and apply it to a given scenario in an exam question.

Typical mistake

Many candidates mention irrelevant user groups in their answer to exam question scenarios, which means relatively easy marks are lost.

Now test yourself

TESTED

1 A sports facility introduces a new exercise class at 3 p.m. on Wednesdays and Fridays.
  a) Identify **two** user groups who are likely to be able to participate in this class. [2 marks]
  b) Identify **two** user groups who are unlikely to be able to participate in this class. [2 marks]
2 Which of the following is **not** a user group experiencing limited access to sport? [1 mark]
  a) People from ethnic minority backgrounds
  b) Unemployed people
  c) People with disabilities
  d) People who are employed/economically secure

Barriers that affect participation in sport and solutions to such barriers

A barrier to participation is something that stops or limits an individual from participating or developing in a physical activity or sport. Attitudes, assumptions and ignorance can be just as much a problem as not having opportunities or the ability to get involved.

Ethnic minorities

REVISED

People from ethnic minorities often face a number of barriers to participation, meaning that they are less likely to be involved in sports or certain activities. Such barriers include:

- a lack of ethnic minority **role models** to encourage participation
- a lack of awareness or information about what is currently available
- limited provision or lack of appealing activities which meet their needs
- fear of **discrimination** or **racism**
- possible language barriers
- **cultural norms** (e.g. traditional gender roles, encouragement to focus on academic studies rather than sport)
- religious reasons (e.g. Muslim women may choose not to show certain parts of their body or participate in sport with or in front of men).

Possible solutions to barriers to participation include:

- promoting role models from ethnic minority backgrounds
- employing coaches, commentators and participants from ethnic minority backgrounds
- advertising and promotion of activities specifically targeted to ethnic minority groups
- providing appropriate activity options that may appeal to ethnic minority communities
- enforcing anti-discrimination laws and zero tolerance of racism and hate speech
- producing schedules, signs and advertising materials in different languages; providing translators and interpreters
- respecting cultural and religious norms and **religious observances** via flexible provision, including single-sex and women-only sessions.

> **Role model**: A person viewed by others as an example to be imitated.
>
> **Discrimination**: The unjust treatment of different categories of people based on characteristics such as ethnicity, sex or disability.
>
> **Racism**: Prejudice, discrimination or antagonism directed against someone of a different race or ethnicity based on the belief that one's own ethnic background is superior.
>
> **Cultural norms**: The standards by which we live – the rules and expectations of society.
>
> **Religious observances**: Behaviour in relation to religious customs (e.g. some religious people may not practise sport on certain days of the week, such as Sunday).

> **Exam tip**
>
> Make sure you understand the relevant barriers and can specifically link them to the experiences of ethnic minority groups, for example, 'a lack of BAME role models' rather than just 'a lack of role models'. You should also include fear of discrimination and restrictions experienced resulting from language/cultural barriers.

Figure 1.2 Jess and her father in *Bend It Like Beckham* (2002)

Revision activity

In the film *Bend It Like Beckham* (2002), the main character, Jess, is a teenage girl from an orthodox Sikh background who rebels against her parents' traditional views and joins a football team. Her parents (particularly her mother) are against her playing football. Write a list of the barriers to participation faced by Jess.

Typical mistake

When answering questions linked to barriers for ethnic minority groups, do not include irrelevant answers such as cost/lack of money, lack of time and lack of transport, unless it is suggested in the question, as these barriers can apply to any group.

Now test yourself

TESTED

A married couple moved to Britain from India six months ago. Both individuals would like to do more sporting activity.

1 Identify **three** barriers to participation which could affect their participation. [3 marks]
2 Suggest **three** strategies which could be used to try and overcome these barriers. [3 marks]

Retired people or people over the age of 50

REVISED

Barriers to participation in sport faced by **retired people** and those aged over 50 include:

- lack of income/disposable income: for people who have retired and are no longer earning an income, the costs of participation in sport may become a barrier. Such costs include purchasing equipment, membership or entrance fees and transport costs to sporting venues

- lack of mobility or fitness due to long periods of inactivity and/or the increased likelihood of health issues such as osteoporosis, diabetes and high blood pressure will negatively impact on participation

- lack of accessibility to sports facilities and equipment (e.g. no public transport or suitable gym machines)

- few positive 50+ role models to encourage participation

- lack of awareness and information about what is currently available to retired and older people

- limited provision or lack of appealing activities which meet the specific needs of older people

Retired people: Individuals who have withdrawn from their active working life and are no longer employed in an occupation.

- lack of time, because an individual is still working full-time or is caring for grandchildren, limiting their availability for participation in sport
- lack of self-esteem and confidence or anxiety over their ability relative to younger, more able participants.

Possible solutions to barriers to participation include:

- decreasing or subsidising the cost of participation
- promoting schemes aimed at encouraging participation among older people (e.g. the **Free Swimming Programme** aimed at the 60+ age group, as well as community-based initiatives)
- providing access to medical advice prior to participation and continuing to monitor as appropriate via visits to health practitioners
- providing free transport or cheaper access to public transport
- using suitably aged/50+ role models to encourage participation
- advertising and targeted promotion of activities specifically to retired people and those over 50 in venues and places most likely to be accessed by the 50+ age group (e.g. libraries and community centres)
- offering taster sessions to new participants or for new activities
- providing appropriate and appealing activity options for older people (e.g. activities adapted to suit older people's health and fitness levels, as well as activities specifically designed to increase participation among older people, such as recreational walking, bowls and **walking football**)
- providing more flexible programming of sessions for older people, including sessions aimed exclusively at the over 50s.

> **Free Swimming Programme**: A Sport England initiative (no longer offered on a nationwide basis) that was designed to increase participation in swimming in England, leading to improved health and economic benefits. The initiative was based around local authorities providing free swimming for children aged 16 and under and people over 60 years of age.
>
> **Walking football**: An adaptation of association football aimed at getting people aged over 50 involved in playing football. The rules have been adapted and include no running and only limited contact.

Exam tip

If an exam question asks you to outline or describe barriers to participation for retired people or those over the age of 50, make sure you can expand on each of the examples given above in order to access maximum marks. For example, when explaining lack of time as a potential barrier to the over 50s participating in sport, you should mention that people over 50 may still be working and/or spending time looking after grandchildren.

Revision activity

Read the Age UK 'Fit as a Fiddle' publication (see link below) to find out more about barriers and solutions to participation in sport for older people and the ways in which activities can be adapted to accommodate their specific needs.

www.activityalliance.org.uk/assets/000/000/249/Fit_as_a_fiddle_resource_original.pdf?1462830235

Typical mistake

When outlining solutions to lack of participation by retired people/the 50+ age group, many candidates' answers are too brief and are not specifically linked to this user group. For example, 'lack of role models' is too vague – instead say 'lack of suitable elderly role models'.

Now test yourself

TESTED

Tom is 65 years old and retired, with only his state pension as income. He has low self-esteem that has caused him to be physically inactive for a long time.

1 Suggest **three** strategies that could be used to try and overcome the barriers to participation which Tom faces. [3 marks]
2 Identify **three** barriers to participation in sport faced by retired people and those aged over 50. [3 marks]

Families with young children

Barriers that may restrict the participation in sport of families with young children include:

- lack of disposable income: increased expenses for families with children mean that participation may become unaffordable (e.g. purchasing equipment for children and membership or entrance fees)
- parents' lack of free time, perhaps due to work commitments
- existing **family commitments** and parents trying to do other activities with their young children
- lack of awareness of available activities, due to a lack of advertising
- lack of childcare provision and high costs of childcare
- adults and parents feeling too tired.

Possible solutions to barriers to participation include:

- decreasing or subsidising the costs of participation by promoting schemes aimed at families with young children, e.g. family discount membership schemes, holiday clubs
- advertising sport using role models that women and girls can relate to
- planning sessions at times that can accommodate restrictions due to work and school commitments (e.g. mid-morning sessions when older children have been dropped off at school and energy levels are still relatively high; summer holiday activities for the whole family)
- advertising sport sessions in places that families with young children access on a regular basis (e.g. nurseries, schools and play centres)
- programming fun activity sessions which parents and young children can join in with
- promoting participation via specialist campaigns, such as Sport England's 'This Girl Can'. This campaign has been promoted via TV, cinemas and social media using the hashtag #thisgirlcan and shows ordinary women and girls participating in sport, enabling this target group to identify with role models who are 'just like them'
- providing free **crèche facilities** or access to childcare at sport and leisure facilities.

> **Family commitments:** Parents' and care givers' responsibilities and willingness to try to meet the varied needs of their children and each other.

> **Crèche facilities:** A nursery where young children are cared for (e.g. during a working day or while their parent is participating in sport/physical activity at a leisure centre).

Figure 1.3 Baby swimming class

Exam tip

In an exam question, barriers linked to families and family commitments may be focused on women or ask you to consider their experiences as part of your answer. This is because women often face additional barriers to participation, despite improvements in access and awareness in recent years.

Typical mistake

Some candidates automatically describe barriers linked to cost as a reason why families with young children do not participate in sport, even when the scenario given in the exam question describes a family where both parents work (i.e. both adults in the family are earning money, making cost less of a barrier). Remember: not all barriers are applicable for every group.

Now test yourself

TESTED

Sue and John are married and in their late 20s. They both work full time and have two young children aged 4 and 6.
1   Identify the user group referred to in the information above.   [1 mark]
2   Identify **three** barriers Sue is likely to face which may affect her participation in sport.   [3 marks]

Single parents

REVISED

Barriers to participation that single parents may face include:
- lack of activities that the child/children and the single parent can enjoy together (particularly if there are large age differences between the children and therefore different interests)
- restrictions on available time due to working hours
- lack of time, perhaps due to family commitments such as taking older children to school, etc.
- activities that are not accessible
- lack of appealing or suitable activities and programmed sessions
- little disposable income and high participation costs (membership fees, transport costs, equipment)
- fewer role models of parents raising a family alone, especially female role models for single mothers
- lack of childcare availability to enable participation in sport and exercise
- lack of awareness of what is available
- no suitable facilities in the local area.

Some solutions to these barriers include:

- programming fun activity sessions which the parent and young child/children can join in with, for example, the Change 4 Life '10 Minute Shake Up' games
- promoting schemes aimed at encouraging participation of single parents with young children (e.g. family discount membership schemes)
- decreasing or subsidising participation costs
- planning sessions at times to accommodate single parents' lack of time or to overcome restrictions due to work commitments (e.g. when children are at school and parents' energy levels may still be relatively high)
- advertising sessions to increase awareness in places that single parents with young children access on a regular basis, such as nurseries, schools and play centres
- promoting participation via specialist campaigns (e.g. Sport England's 'This Girl Can') and using role models that show ordinary men and women taking part in sport
- providing free crèche facilities or access to childcare at sport and leisure centres.

Revision activity

Visit the Sport England website (see link below) and watch the advert for '10 Minute Shake Ups', which shows how parents can make activity fun for their young children.

www.sportengland.org/news-and-features/news/2019/july/4/change4life-and-disney-uk-launch-new-10-minute-shake-ups/

Exam tip

When answering an exam question about barriers to participation, you must specifically link your answer to the user group identified or described in the question. For example, in the case of barriers faced by single parents, simply stating 'lack of transport' is too vague; lack of transport is a barrier because of cost and so you must make the link clear in order to gain a mark.

Typical mistake

When writing an answer to an exam question, avoid repeating information already provided in the question as this will not gain you any marks.

Now test yourself

TESTED ☐

Maria is a non-working single parent with two young children, who wants to be as fit and active as possible.

Identify **three** barriers that might prevent Maria from regularly taking part in physical activity or sport.

[3 marks]

Children

Children in their pre-teenage years are the fifth user group identified in the specification. Barriers to participation include:

- lack of income or disposable income: if a child's family cannot afford the costs of participation (e.g. transport, equipment, entry fees or lesson costs), participation is unlikely
- lack of interest or motivation: other interests are more important to some children than sport
- poor provision, such as restricted times when children are able to participate
- limited awareness of available activities
- the requirement for supervision by an adult such as a parent or guardian: if unavailable, children will be unable to participate
- access to sports facilities, perhaps due to reliance on others for transport or age limits
- poor self-image or a lack of confidence: some children are highly self-conscious when comparing their sporting ability relative to other children
- lack of sporting role models or parental encouragement to participate
- limited or unappealing school provision
- limited availability of coaches or coaching sessions to develop skills and techniques.

Solutions to these challenges include:

- decreasing or subsidising the costs of participation, for example, by promoting schemes aimed at encouraging participation among children, such as **Sportivate**
- providing fun and appealing activities to motivate children to participate more
- using suitable role models to encourage participation (e.g. children's TV presenters)
- increasing the flexibility of sports provision for children (e.g. adapting equipment and pitch size to suit the age group)
- promoting participation opportunities for children via **social media**
- planning provision to develop different abilities and confidence levels (e.g. beginners' classes, single sex provision)
- using positive role models children can relate to
- educating parents on the benefits of sport and physical activity for their children
- improving school provision (e.g. via **school–club links** and taster sessions which give a flavour of an activity; after-school clubs and holiday sport courses; running gender-specific sessions such as girls only and increasing advertising in schools)
- training coaches to meet the specific needs of coaching children (e.g. via Sports Coach UK courses).

Sportivate: A Sport England/National Lottery funded programme which ended in 2017, but which aimed to get more 11–25-year olds involved in sport and physical activity.

Social media: Websites and computer programs that allow people to communicate and share information via the internet using a computer or mobile phone.

School–club links: An agreement between a school and a community-based sports club to work together to meet the needs of young people.

LO1 Understand the issues which affect participation in sport

Figure 1.4 Children taking part in a dance class

Now test yourself

Many parents and teachers are concerned that children in their early years of secondary
school are not physically active enough.
1 State **three** possible barriers which may prevent children from being physically active.   [3 marks]
2 Identify **three** strategies a secondary school could use to enable children to participate more regularly in physical activity. [3 marks]

Teenagers

REVISED

Barriers faced by people aged 13–19 years old may include:

● lack of disposable income: some teenagers and their families cannot afford the costs of participation, e.g. transport costs, lesson costs, cost of purchasing equipment, membership/entrance fees

● lack of time due to other commitments (e.g. as a result of the demands of education or, for older teenagers, employment)

● access to sports facilities as teenagers may still need to rely on others for transport

● lack of role models in certain sports to encourage participation, or a lack of parental encouragement to participate

● limited PE or sports club provision (e.g. restricted times when teenagers are able to participate in school PE programmes and/or at local sports clubs)

● limited awareness of facilities and activities available to participate in

● lack of interest and poor motivation: some teenagers cannot be bothered or feel studying is more important than sport; other leisure pursuits are more appealing, such as playing computer games or using social media

- embarrassment/negative body image/lack of confidence: teenagers may be highly self-conscious, especially when comparing their sporting ability to others in their age group
- peer pressure – participating in sport may not be seen as 'cool'.

Possible solutions to such barriers include:

- decreasing or subsidising the costs of participation or offering concessions
- promoting schemes aimed at encouraging participation among teenagers (e.g. Sportivate/Free Swimming Programme)
- providing more activities held at school/after school
- providing free or subsidised transport to sport facilities
- using active, healthy role models to encourage participation (e.g. via schemes such as **Youth Sport Trust Athlete Mentors**)
- increasing motivation by promoting the health benefits of activity and providing activities which are fun and appealing to teenagers, e.g. skate boarding, dodgeball
- building confidence through educational initiatives and media campaigns
- promoting participation opportunities for teenagers via social media
- planning provision to develop ability and confidence (e.g. beginners' classes; single sex provision)
- using positive role models who teenagers can relate to and educating parents and teenagers on the benefits of sport and physical activity
- improving school provision (e.g. via school–club links/taster sessions which give a flavour of an activity; after-school clubs/holiday sport courses offering appealing activities; increased advertising in schools).

> **Youth Sport Trust Athlete Mentors**: A scheme that involves using some of Britain's most successful athletes to visit schools and inspire young people to get involved in sport.

Revision activity

Write down five barriers to participation for teenagers from the list above and then from memory try to match them directly to appropriate solutions.

Exam tip

An exam question may ask you to write a specific number of points, e.g. 'Identify **three** barriers to participation for teenagers.' Make sure you only give the required number of answers and avoid repeating yourself or making points that are too similar, e.g. avoid stating 'lack of time' as your first point and 'school commitments' as your second.

Now test yourself   TESTED ☐

Some teenagers feel unable to become more physically active because of high costs and lack of time due to schoolwork and exam commitments.

Suggest **two** ways to overcome these barriers to participation for teenagers.   [2 marks]

People with disabilities

People with disabilities often face extra challenges when trying to participate in sport. Barriers to participation include:

- high costs of accessible transport and specialist equipment, as well as general costs relating to membership or entry fees
- poor accessibility at sports facilities
- poor provision of adapted or specialist equipment or difficulties accessing it
- lack of specialist facilities that meet the specific needs of individuals with disabilities
- availability of adapted or suitable transport (not all public transport is accessible and people with certain disabilities may need to be driven or assisted)
- lack of visibility of sportspeople or role models with disabilities to encourage participation and/or a negative portrayal of people with disabilities in the media
- lack of advertising/information about what is currently available for people with disabilities
- limited provision or a lack of appealing activities that meet the specific needs of people with disabilities (e.g. visual impairment and/or physical impairment)
- lack of confidence/low self-esteem due to concerns and anxieties over access issues or ability to participate
- discrimination or fear of discrimination.

Figure 1.5 Access equipment in a sports context

Ways to overcome barriers to participation for people with disabilities include:

- subsidising the costs of participation (e.g. offering free swimming for participants and their carers)
- improving access to facilities (e.g. ramps/access doors/hearing loops/accessible parking close to an entrance)
- providing adapted equipment and facilities (e.g. specialist goal ball for people who are blind/partially blind; hoists and pool wheelchairs to enable access to swimming pools)

- providing appropriate transport (e.g. a wheelchair-accessible minibus or taxi to and from activity sessions)
- using role models with disabilities (e.g. Paralympians) in advertising campaigns and employing coaches with disabilities to encourage participation
- advertising/targeted promotion of activities specifically to people with disabilities and providing information in a variety of accessible formats (e.g. Braille)
- providing suitable programmed sessions or adapted activity options (e.g. activities/programmes specifically designed to increase participation among specific groups, such as **Boccia**; providing separate activity sessions for people with disabilities)
- providing separate sessions with specialist coaches to meet the specific needs/varied ability levels of individuals with disabilities.

> **Boccia**: A target sport, involving soft leather balls, that is played indoors by athletes who need high levels of support.

Revision activity

Consider the solutions to barriers to participation for people with disabilities and make a list of practical examples of how they can be applied (e.g. making physical assistance available to improve access to a facility). Remember: there are many types of disability and not all are visible.

Typical mistake

When asked to describe barriers for individuals with disabilities, students often state lack of money. This is not sufficient on its own, as lack of money is a barrier to many groups. Instead, you will need to demonstrate your understanding of the specific experiences of people with particular disabilities, for example, specially adapted equipment or transport is often expensive, making it difficult for people to afford.

Exam tip

If an exam question asks you to *outline* barriers to participation, do not give a one-word answer. The command word 'outline' means you should write a detailed answer to fully illustrate your knowledge of the points you are making.

Now test yourself

TESTED

Using examples, describe **two** ways a sport of your choice can be made more accessible for people with disabilities. [4 marks]

Unemployed/economically disadvantaged people

REVISED

People who are unemployed or have a low income may be less likely to participate in sport. Barriers to participation include:

- limited disposable income: people who are unemployed or in poorly paid jobs will have little money to spare and so may not prioritise sport or be able to afford the costs involved in participation (e.g. equipment and membership fees)
- lack of transport (e.g. car ownership or the cost of public transport to facilities may be too expensive)
- poor availability of activities (e.g. a lack of local facilities)
- lack of awareness of activities that are subsidised or provided free of charge
- lack of time (e.g. due to spending time looking for a job, working in more than one job or working long hours on minimum wage)
- lack of motivation due to low levels of confidence/self-esteem.

Possible solutions to barriers to participation include:

- promoting discounted or free activities (e.g. subsidised classes at leisure centres and participation in free activities such as walking or jogging)
- subsidising costs associated with participation (e.g. transport and activity costs)
- increased advertising of activities and sports that are available in the local area (e.g. via **Doorstep Sport**)
- providing activity options linked to the needs of unemployed/ economically disadvantaged people (e.g. specifically designed activities/ programmes such as those set up by **StreetGames**).

Doorstep Sport: Sport club programme (set up by StreetGames) which supports disadvantaged young people to participate in sport.

StreetGames: National sports charity that seeks to make sport more widely available for young people in disadvantaged areas.

Revision activity

Find out more about solutions to barriers to participation for people who are unemployed/economically disadvantaged via the Sport England and StreetGames websites:

www.sportengland.org

www.streetgames.org

Working singles/couples

Barriers to participation in sport for **working singles/couples** include:
- long working hours
- lack of free time (e.g. due to work commitments)
- lack of disposable income/high participation costs (e.g. membership fees/equipment costs)
- lack of awareness regarding availability of facilities and activities
- limited activity provision to meet their requirements.

Working singles/couples: Young adults who have work commitments and no children.

HIIT: High Intensity Interval Training.

Possible solutions to barriers to participation include:

- planning physical activity to fit in with busy daily lives (e.g. scheduling sessions before work or at lunchtimes; offering an intensive activity in a short amount of time, such as 10-minute **HIIT** sessions)
- decreasing or subsidising the costs of participation
- promoting schemes that encourage participation in activities which are free and that can be done at any time, such as walking or jogging; offering free fitness apps on mobile phones
- advertising sessions to increase awareness in places that working singles/couples access on a regular basis (e.g. public transport/billboards on major roads)
- encouraging participation via work-based sessions or group activities with like-minded individuals (i.e. create a socially appealing activity to encourage participation).

Revision activity

Make brief notes on three types of activity that a person with limited time for sports and exercise could do.

Figure 1.6 Phone fitness apps are useful tools for monitoring fitness and increasing motivation

Typical mistake

When asked to outline solutions for a lack of participation by working singles/couples linked to lack of time, avoid simply writing 'find more time'. A better answer would be 'plan to do physical activity early in the morning to fit in with a busy lifestyle'.

The factors which can impact upon the popularity of sport in the UK

REVISED

Participation levels

- Sports where there is a strong **infrastructure** in place are likely to have widespread appeal and mass participation.
- Increased awareness of the importance of health and fitness has meant lots of fitness clubs are now available, offering activities such as circuit training, Pilates and yoga.

Infrastructure: The facilities and systems that serve a particular area of a country or city/town, such as roads, schools, public spaces and leisure facilities.

Provision

- Provision includes access to facilities to enable participation in sport.
- If sporting facilities such as football/rugby pitches and leisure centres are readily available, it will encourage participation in sport, but if accessibility is more limited, then fewer people will get involved.
- The ability to swim is an important life skill, which also helps to develop health and fitness. Swimming can be encouraged via government and local authority investment in good quality provision, i.e. funding local swimming pools throughout the UK.

Environment/climate

- Where you live can affect access to some activities (e.g. those living in towns and cities may have limited or no access to outdoor/water sports facilities).

- There are costs involved in hiring facilities if no natural resources are available (e.g. indoor rock climbing).

- Travel to access sport and leisure facilities can involve a lengthy journey or high costs, which may negatively impact on participation.

- Fewer people participate in outdoor sports during bad weather.

- Frequent interruptions to play due to bad weather can lead to a loss of interest (e.g. in cricket).

- Weather restrictions lead to a shortened season (e.g. cricket).

- The climate limits the availability of activities in some areas of the UK (e.g. snow sports are more accessible in Scotland).

- All-weather/**4G pitches** have improved accessibility to sports like hockey and football even when the weather is poor.

> **4G pitches**: Synthetic sport surface; also known as an all-weather pitch.

Spectatorship/media coverage

- Watching a sport (in person or on television) or listening to sport on the radio can encourage people to want to take part themselves.

- Watching a favourite team or sporting hero live (e.g. for cyclists, watching the Tour de Yorkshire) can help inspire more people to participate in a sport.

- A lack of opportunity to watch a sport live can negatively impact on participation. For instance, squash and volleyball are rarely viewed live in large numbers, partly because they receive very little media coverage.

- However, increased spectatorship can also have a negative impact on participation, if people focus more on watching professionals play than on playing a sport themselves.

- Media coverage raises the profile of a sport, increasing awareness of it and therefore the likelihood of people choosing to participate in it.

- Free-to-air coverage of a sport via a **terrestrial TV station** or via radio gives access to a far bigger audience than if a sport is only shown on subscription channels such as **Sky Sports** and BT Sport.

- The Wimbledon tennis championships and the Olympic Games are televised on the BBC in the UK as a free-to-air channel, while cricket (e.g. the Ashes) is currently only available to watch via Sky Sports, which is a subscription-based channel. The rights to broadcast the UEFA Champions League football coverage are held by BT Sport.

- Some argue that broadcasting sports on anything other than free-to-air television is negative as it automatically limits access to the sport, especially to certain groups.

- However, it can also be said that Sky Sports has had a positive influence on the coverage of sports which receive limited coverage on terrestrial TV, such as netball. This may positively influence opportunities to participate in a sport at the elite level.

- Increased media coverage of a sport generates more income via sponsorship opportunities and media rights, which can then be invested into providing further opportunities to participate in the sport. For example, the England and Wales Cricket Board (ECB), which is the governing body of cricket in England and Wales, invests income from media coverage into the management and development of all forms of cricket for both male and female participants, from junior levels up to international standard.

> **Terrestrial TV stations**: Free-to-air TV, such as BBC, ITV, Channel 4 and Channel 5 in the UK.
>
> **Sky Sports**: Main subscription-based sports channel provider in the UK.

Success for teams and individuals

- When a team is successful at a major sporting event, it can inspire and encourage participation in that sport. For example, the England netball team won gold at the Commonwealth Games in 2018, while the England cricket team won the World Cup in 2019 in a game which finished with a tie-break 'super over'. This has resulted in more people becoming interested in these sports.
- Individual success can also serve as a source of inspiration for people to aspire to; the Tour de France success of Chris Froome and Geraint Thomas is one of the reasons why more people are taking up road cycling.

Role models

- Having positive role models to aspire to can encourage people to take up sport, while a lack of them can be a negative factor that means people are less likely to participate.
- The lack of positive role models to aspire to is seen as a common cause of lower participation rates for particular user groups, such as the relative lack of British Asian football players or high-profile females in sports such as cricket and rugby.

Acceptability

- Some sports have a particular **culture** that negatively influences participation in that sport. For instance, boxing has been criticised for causing injury to the participants during the normal course of competition, as the sport involves punching an opponent.
- Sports can also have negative associations with certain behaviours, e.g. weightlifting and steroid abuse or football and hooliganism.

> **Culture:** The rules, customs and beliefs of a particular group or society.

> **Exam tip**
>
> You will need to know and be able to link various factors influencing the popularity of a sport in the UK to relevant sporting examples in order to illustrate the point you are making.

> **Revision activity**
>
> Locate where you live on an online map and then view what facilities are available to encourage participation in sport within a five-mile radius of your home.

> **Typical mistake**
>
> If an exam question asks you to evaluate or discuss the impact of factors affecting participation in sports, remember to include both negative and positive points. If you only given one set of points, you will limit the marks available to you.

> **Now test yourself** `TESTED` ☐
>
> Identify **three** factors (other than media coverage and role models) that can have an impact upon the popularity of sport in the UK. [3 marks]

Current UK trends in the popularity of different sports

Sport England is a public organisation whose role is to work both nationally and locally to build the foundations of community sports in England. It regularly publishes research and measures participation in sport and physical activity in England via the Active Lives surveys, which describe activity levels across England. Active Lives Adult is published twice a year, while Active Lives Children and Young People is published once a year.

According to the most recent Active Lives Adult Survey:

● The number of people walking for leisure and travel grew to 34.9 million in this period.

● Adventure sports (hill and mountain walking, climbing and orienteering) saw significant growth.

● Fitness activities, driven by gym sessions, are the most popular activity after walking. Within this category, yoga and Pilates grew in popularity, while fitness classes like Zumba became less popular.

● Swimming levels have stabilised after a period of decline. There were peaks in outdoor and open water swimming during the summer heatwave of 2018.

● Weight training sessions have grown in popularity for women.

● Overall cycling levels have dropped, with outdoor, road cycling and racing participation down. However, indoor bike sessions saw a spike.

In the report, Sport England pointed out that the nation's activity habits are changing, which means that the sports sector must become more flexible and be led by public demand to ensure it offers consumers the convenience they seek and activities that are enjoyable, affordable and accessible.

Source: *Active Lives Adult Survey*, May *18/19 Report* (published October 2019)

Popular sports within the UK

Two of the sports that enjoy relatively high popularity in the UK are given below, together with reasons for their popularity.

Football

● Relatively cheap or free to access places in which to play, such as parks and recreation grounds.

● Simple to do, with relatively little specialist equipment needed.

● Many clubs offering facilities/coaches/competitions are available.

● Can be played in most weather conditions.

● High levels of media coverage and popular role models encourage participation.

● Lots of opportunities within school PE programmes.

Swimming

● Relatively cheap (especially if swimming in the sea or open water).

● Good availability of pools in most areas.

● Easy to do alone.

- Non-weight bearing activity so can be a lifelong sporting activity that is good for maintaining health and fitness.
- Plenty of positive role models (e.g. Adam Peaty, Rebecca Adlington, Ellie Simmonds).

Two sports that are less popular in terms of participation are given below, together with reasons why.

Tennis

- Relatively expensive (e.g. court hire/club membership fees).
- Harder to access areas for play (e.g. indoor courts) than areas for other sports.
- Negative impact of climate/poor weather on outdoor courts.
- Lack of provision in school PE programmes.

Golf

- Expensive to access (e.g. golf club membership).
- Requires a large amount of equipment to participate.
- Golf clubs can be difficult to access (e.g. if exclusive to members and not near public transport).
- Lack of provision in school PE programmes.
- Negative impact of climate/poor weather.

Exam tip

Be prepared to answer data-related questions on trends in popularity of certain sports.

Revision activity

Keep up to date with the latest trends in the popularity of different sports in England by viewing the most recent Active Lives statistics at: www.sportengland.org/research/active-lives-survey

Typical mistake

Avoid losing marks in the exam by making sure you link your answers to the data/information provided in the question stem.

Now test yourself

TESTED

The table shows the number of adult participants in two sports for the periods May 2017–18 and May 2018–19.

	Swimming	Racket sports (e.g. tennis)
May 17/18	4.5 million	2.2 million
May 18/19	4.7 million	2.1 million

Source: Active Lives Adult Survey, May 18/19 Report (published October 2019)

Using the data above, give **two** reasons to account for the recent trends in:
a) swimming [2 marks]
b) racket sports. [2 marks]

The growth of new and emerging sports and activities in the UK

REVISED ☐

New and emerging sports and activities are becoming more popular and seeking to establish themselves in the UK. Some examples include:

- ultimate frisbee
- footgolf
- **korfball**
- handball
- **futsal**.

An emerging sport can be made more popular by:

- encouraging more people to do it
- providing suitable facilities/pitches/equipment
- providing more competitions
- training more coaches/officials
- increasing the number of clubs available to join
- increased media coverage and the use of role models to encourage participation
- advertising and promotion
- holding competitive matches to encourage spectatorship
- offering taster sessions/subsidised coaching sessions
- adapting the sport for different user groups (e.g. non-contact)
- offering the sport in school PE programmes (e.g. either as part of the curriculum or as an extra-curricular activity)
- organising **grassroots** schemes to encourage participation in physical activity at the lowest, most local level for health, educational or social purposes.

Futsal is an example of an emerging sport in the UK. Some of the reasons why it is increasing in popularity are shown below.

- It can be played indoors, so can be played all year round, and indoor facilities can be adapted quite easily to suit play.
- It is accessible to different levels, ages and abilities, as it is easier to play than 11-a-side association football.
- It is useful in developing skills for association football.
- Matches are shorter, so it can be played in reduced time periods, which suits the lifestyle of some participants (e.g. working people).
- More competitive opportunities are becoming available.
- There is now greater promotion of futsal.
- Players experience more involvement in the game and contact with the ball compared to football.

Padel tennis is an example of an emerging sport that may also help to increase interest in playing tennis. It is a mix of tennis and squash played on a court approximately half the size of a traditional court, with a walled edge and using modified equipment. Padel tennis can be played indoors or outdoors.

> **Korfball**: A ball sport with similarities to netball and basketball played by two teams of eight players (four male and four female), with the aim of throwing the ball into a net.
>
> **Futsal**: A variation on association football (soccer) played on a hard court with a smaller/low bounce ball.

> **Grassroots**: The most basic level of an organisation (e.g. local non-league football clubs, as opposed to elite football clubs such as Arsenal or Barcelona FC).

The following factors may explain its popularity:

- It is easy to play as the ball strike is close to the hand/body.
- It is rewarding to learn as players' skills can accelerate rapidly.
- It is very sociable as it is always played in doubles.
- It can be played by people with varying fitness levels.
- It can be flexible in terms of time and space.

Figure 1.7 **Padel tennis**

Exam tip

Be prepared to outline ways in which an emerging sport can increase its popularity in the UK.

Revision activity

Identify an emerging sport available to participate in close to where you live and investigate how it is trying to attract more people to play.

Typical mistake

When describing emerging sports, do not give an incorrect example, for instance, netball, swimming, rounders and athletics are all established sports and would not gain any marks.

Now test yourself   TESTED ☐

1 Which of the following would be classed as an emerging sport in the UK?   [1 mark]
   a) Athletics
   b) Netball
   c) Rounders
   d) Ultimate frisbee
2 Explain why the emerging sport known as futsal has become more popular in recent years.   [4 marks]

LO2 Know about the role of sport in promoting values

Values which can be promoted through sport

Participating in sport has many benefits:

- **Team spirit**: Team members can feel a sense of pride and loyalty that motivates them to support each other and work hard to do their best for the team. For example, in sporting events such as the Davis Cup in tennis, team members work together and support others in achieving a common goal, i.e. winning.

- **Fair play**: Performers are expected to show highly appropriate/polite behaviour. This includes respecting opponents, adhering to the rules and being fair to others when playing sport (e.g. maintaining silence when a rugby player is about to attempt a conversion of a try).

- **Citizenship**: Sport provides people with a chance to act as 'good citizens' by getting involved in their local community (e.g. helping to run local community sports clubs as volunteers or coaches).

- **Tolerance and respect**: Sport is a good way of developing an understanding of different countries and their cultures (e.g. events such as the Commonwealth Games are used to promote mutual tolerance and respect among opponents, including showing respect for another country's national anthem when it is played at a medal ceremony).

- **Inclusion**: There are a variety of schemes and initiatives to get under-represented social groups involved in sport (e.g. 'This Girl Can' is a campaign to get more women involved in sport).

- **National pride**: International sporting events are a good way of promoting a sense of unity in performers and spectators under the flag of a country. It can involve wearing the team kit or the national flag, singing the national anthem and congregating together in large numbers in city centres at open-air events to support the national team.

- **Excellence**: This involves encouraging sports performers to strive to develop themselves to the full and achieve excellence in their favourite sport via consistent top-level performance.

- **Tolerance and respect**: Accepting and welcoming players from different social backgrounds.

- **Social inclusion**: Making sure all community groups have an opportunity to participate in sport.

Figure 1.8 Participants in international sporting events often sing their national anthem

The Olympic and Paralympic movement

- The Olympic and Paralympic movement has a number of important principles associated with it, including the creed, the Olympic symbol and the Olympic and Paralympic values.

- The Olympic creed is a moral message outlining the value of endeavour and trying your best to overcome challenges. It was first spoken by Baron Pierre de Coubertin, the founder of the modern Olympic Games, in 1908:

  'The most important thing is not to win but to take part, just as the most important thing in life is not the triumph but the struggle. The essential thing is not to have conquered, but to have fought well.'

- The Olympic symbol is the five interlocking rings that represent the union of the five continents of the world that take part in the Olympics.

Figure 1.9 The Olympic rings

The Olympic and Paralympic values are defined in Table 1.2.

Table 1.2 Olympic and Paralympic values

Value	Explanation
Respect	Applauding/congratulating opponents at the end of a competition; treating people from all backgrounds with dignity
Excellence	Achieving a personal best in an event; athletes performing to their full potential
Friendship	Making friends with athletes from other countries at the closing ceremony
Courage	Overcoming difficulties to compete in an event
Determination	Overcoming barriers to train and compete (ranging from access difficulties to a lack of self-belief)
Inspiration	Generating excitement in others about a sport or performance and providing role models to others in a similar position
Equality	Championing equal rights (e.g. for women and athletes with disabilities)

Exam tip

The number of answers/points that should be made in answer to an exam question will be shown by the number of marks available. Remember LAMA – Look At Mark Allocation!

Typical mistake

Do not repeat points already made, as this restricts the number of marks you can achieve when answering a question (e.g. 'playing fairly' means the same as 'fair play').

Revision activity

Draw a table and copy the seven Olympic and Paralympic values into one column. Then try to define each of these in turn. Check to see if you have got them all correct.

Now test yourself

TESTED ☐

1 Are the following statements true or false in relation to the Olympic creed?
  a) The most important thing is not the winning but the taking part. [1 mark]
  b) The struggle is more important than the triumph. [1 mark]
2 Identify **two** values associated with the Paralympics. [2 marks]

Other initiatives and events which promote values through sport

Sports initiatives, events and campaigns can be used to promote certain values in those taking part, as shown in Table 1.3.

Table 1.3 Sports initiatives and the values they promote

Initiative	Values promoted
Sport Relief	Citizenship/tolerance and respect: ● An annual public fundraising campaign encouraging people to get active and raise money for vulnerable people in the UK and abroad. ● In 2019, this included a celebrity netball match held during the World Netball Championships.
ECB's 'Chance to Shine' campaign	Team spirit/inclusion: ● A scheme aimed at ensuring cricket continues to be played in state schools ('Chance to Shine Schools') and inner-city areas ('Chance to Shine Street') where children may not have been given the chance to play. ● Links to Cricket Unleashed, the new framework for cricket in England and Wales, which commits the sport to inspiring more people to play and follow the game and to take it into new places and communities. ● One activity of 'Chance to Shine Street' uses a 'tapeball' (a tennis ball wrapped in electrical tape) with plastic bats to play cricket in matches that last for just 20 minutes – it is cricket's equivalent of five-a-side football.
FIFA's 'Football for Hope' campaign	Inclusion: ● A collaboration between FIFA and 'Street Football World' – a social project for disadvantaged people, using football as a focal and unifying point.
Sport England's – 'This Girl Can' campaign	Inclusion: ● A scheme aimed at breaking down barriers to participation for women (e.g. lack of confidence, fear of judgement).
The FA's 'Respect' campaign	Fair play/tolerance and respect: ● This scheme was launched in the 2008/09 football season following an increase in behavioural problems in the game. ● It encourages appropriate behaviour between footballers and, in particular, towards officials during matches. ● The FA's new campaign 'We Only Do Positive' is aimed at coaches and parents within mini-soccer and youth football and is intended to ensure that coaches and parents work towards creating an environment that is safe, inclusive and fun for all players, whatever their age.
Kick It Out	Inclusion: ● Kick It Out is an organisation working to promote equality and inclusion within English football. Its aim is to promote inclusion and eliminate racism and it works to achieve this through involvement in football, education and the community. ● The 'Let's Kick Racism Out of Football' campaign was established by a small independent charity in 1993 following requests from clubs, players and fans to tackle racist attitudes within the game. ● Kick It Out was then established in 1997, having expanded its aims to include all aspects of discrimination, inequality and exclusion.

Revision activity

Visit the Chance to Shine website (www.chancetoshine.org) and research how the 'Chance to Shine Schools' and 'Chance to Shine Street' campaigns are working in schools and local communities to increase team spirit and promote inclusion among disadvantaged people.

Exam tip

Make sure you can link appropriate sporting values to different sporting initiatives/campaigns.

Now test yourself

1 Identify **one** sports initiative and a value it promotes. [1 mark]
2 Link the sports initiative to the relevant sporting value(s) it promotes. [3 marks]

Kick It Out	Team spirit/inclusion
Chance to Shine	Inclusion
Sport Relief	Citizenship/tolerance and respect

The importance of etiquette and sporting behaviour of both performers and spectators

Sports played with a high level of **etiquette** are often admired by spectators. This is due to the positive sporting behaviour observed (e.g. polite and mutually respectful fair play, often referred to as 'sportsmanship').

Etiquette: The unwritten rules concerning player behaviour.

Reasons for observing etiquette and sporting behaviour

Reasons why performers should observe etiquette and positive sporting behaviour include:

- ensures fairness and the achievement of a fair result
- promotes positive values (e.g. respect for others)
- helps to ensure the safety of themselves and their opponents
- sets a good example to young people and provides a positive role model to children
- improves the reputation of the sport and encourages participation in the sport (e.g. rugby union)
- ensures the sporting activity or game is played effectively in a free flowing and enjoyable manner.

Figure 1.10 Shaking hands with an opponent is an example of sporting etiquette

Sportsmanship

Sportsmanship involves adhering to the written rules of sport, but also the unwritten codes of conduct, as illustrated by the examples below:

- applauding the performance or success of an opponent (e.g. playing an inventive shot in tennis; scoring a goal in netball)
- shaking hands with opponents and officials before and after a game
- showing grace and respect at the end of a game, whether you have won or lost
- showing respect to and freely accepting the decisions of officials
- returning the ball to the opposition in football when they have kicked it out because of an injury to one of your team
- leaving the pitch in cricket when you know you are out (rather than being told to).

Gamesmanship

With ever-increasing rewards for winning at stake, some sports performers resort to negative sporting behaviour via their use of **gamesmanship** to gain an advantage over their opponents.

Examples of gamesmanship include:

- delaying a restart to a contest or 'running down the clock' (wasting time) when winning
- over appealing (i.e. excessive complaining) to an official to pressure them into making a decision to benefit your team (e.g. to an umpire in cricket about whether an opposing batsman or batswoman is out)
- taking time out for an injury or bathroom breaks when not required
- grunting loudly in tennis when playing a shot in order to put an opponent off.

> **Gamesmanship:** Bending the rules and stretching them to their absolute limit in order to gain an advantage.

Spectator etiquette

In addition to performers showing etiquette during sporting contests, spectators of such events also need to behave appropriately. Examples of good **spectator etiquette** include:

- being quiet as a tennis player is about to serve, or a golfer is about to putt
- remaining quiet and standing up during the playing of an opposition's national anthem to show tolerance and respect of different countries through sport
- applauding and encouraging good play by the opposition
- respecting and accepting decisions made by officials and not swearing or using aggressive behaviour towards them
- not going onto the pitch/playing area.

> **Spectator etiquette:** The rules or guidelines for spectators at a sporting event.

> **Typical mistake**
>
> Avoid giving irrelevant examples of sporting etiquette, e.g. a player helping an opponent up off the floor after they have fouled them misses the point, because it was poor etiquette to commit the foul in the first place.

> **Exam tip**
>
> Make sure you can give practical examples of etiquette/good sporting behaviour for both performers and spectators.

Now test yourself

1 Which of the following is **not** an example of gamesmanship? [1 mark]
   a) Wasting time towards the end of a game when winning 1–0.
   b) Taking an injury time-out, even when fully fit, during a tennis match.
   c) Over appealing to the umpire in a cricket match.
   d) Shaking hands with opponents at the end of a football match.
2 Give **two** reasons why it is important to maintain the ethic of sportsmanship in modern-day sport. [2 marks]

The use of performance-enhancing drugs in sport

Sports performers may choose to use prohibited performance-enhancing drugs (PEDs) for a variety of reasons, including:

- an overwhelming desire to win or succeed
- pressure from the media/team/nation to win
- pressure from coaches and managers to increase the chances of winning
- to gain money and fame as a result of success
- to improve performance via increased fitness, strength, stamina, etc.
- to improve recovery time from training sessions or injury
- to increase the ability to train longer or harder
- to mask (i.e. cover up) pain
- to lose weight
- to level the playing field because of the belief that others are taking PEDs.

Reasons why PEDs should not be used include:

- risk of long-term damage to physical and/or mental health, including addiction or over-reliance on PEDs
- negative consequences of being found guilty (e.g. a ban from competing)
- financial penalties imposed on those found guilty (e.g. loss of prize money and loss of sponsorship)
- an unfair advantage over 'clean athletes' who have not taken PEDs
- it is cheating and against the rules of sport
- it gives a sport a bad reputation and can lead to a mistrust of results (e.g. cycling and athletics have both experienced negative publicity regarding drug use by athletes)
- it reflects badly on an individual and their nation.

World Anti-Doping Agency

The **World Anti-Doping Agency (WADA)** aims to ensure a drug-free sporting environment across the world. Its main activities are scientific research, education, development of anti-doping methods and monitoring of the **World Anti-Doping Code**.

The 'Whereabouts rule' is a WADA strategy that tries to ensure a drug-free sporting environment. It involves information that must be provided to the authorities (e.g. the International Sport Federation (IF) or **UK Anti-Doping (UKAD)**) by select groups of elite athletes.

World Anti-Doping Agency (WADA): A foundation initiated by the International Olympic Committee based in Canada to promote, coordinate and monitor the fight against drugs in sports.

World Anti-Doping Code: Published by the World Anti-Doping Agency (WADA), the Code aims to ensure that anti-doping policies, rules and regulations within sport organisations and public authorities are the same throughout the world.

UK Anti-Doping (UKAD): The national anti-doping organisation in the United Kingdom.

According to the Whereabouts rule, selected athletes must be available for random testing at any time. Elite athletes must therefore:

- provide information about their location (outside of competitions)
- provide information about their overnight accommodation
- provide details of their training and competition schedule
- be available for a 60-minute timeslot in an agreed place every day
- understand that three missed tests in a year will result in a sanction.

Testing methods

Testing methods used to try to catch out athletes who are using illegal PEDs include collecting samples of athletes' blood or urine (and sometimes hair or nails), under supervision, to be tested in a laboratory.

Current initiatives

The battle against illegal PEDs is ongoing and involves a variety of different initiatives to try to keep sport drug free. For example:

- creation of partnerships such as cross-organisation work between WADA and national anti-doping organisations such as UK Anti-Doping (UKAD)
- random drugs testing and implementation of the Whereabouts rule
- harsher punishments for those found guilty of taking illegal PEDs (e.g. long-term bans)
- educating performers on the health risks of taking PEDs and creating an ethically fair and drug-free approach to competing (e.g. via UKAD's **100% me** programme)
- loss of sponsorship/National Lottery funding if an athlete is found guilty of taking PEDs.

Drug offences by elite performers

There have been many high-profile drug offences committed by elite sports performers. Many of these are from the world of athletics (e.g. sprinters such as Dwain Chambers) and cycling (e.g. David Millar). **Anabolic steroids** and **EPO (erythropoietin)** are two PEDs that have been used by many.

Elite performers, such as those identified above, have suffered a number of consequences as a result of their actions, including:

- suspension or a long-term ban from competing professionally
- damage to their reputation – the athlete will always be viewed as a cheat
- loss of income and sponsorship
- loss of medals or deletion of records.

Impact of drug taking on the reputation of sport

As well as affecting the reputation of an individual athlete, doping scandals in sport can have a wider impact:

- The sport may gain a negative reputation or image.
- There may be a reduction in income and sponsorship for the sport.
- Spectators may mistrust results and question whether they are watching 'clean' and fair sport.
- A mistrust of a particular sporting event due to the large numbers of positive tests or drug scandals (e.g. 100 m Olympic sprint, the Tour de France).

100% me: UK Anti-Doping's education and information programme to help athletes retain an ethically fair, drug-free approach to sport.

Anabolic steroids: Prescription-only medicines that are sometimes taken without medical advice to increase muscle mass and improve athletic performance.

EPO (erythropoietin): A hormone naturally produced by the kidneys that can be produced artificially and injected to improve the performance of athletes such as cyclists.

- Scepticism about all performers, regardless of whether an individual has been involved in drug taking, due to lots of PED cases in that sport.
- Decreased participation in a sport, especially as young people may be put off taking up the sport.

Ethical issues related to drug taking

Ethics are the moral principles that lead people to behave in the way they do. The use of illegal PEDs is generally viewed as immoral and unethical, although some people from sports governing bodies argue that PEDs should be allowed. Table 1.4 summarises possible reasons for and against allowing the use of PEDs in sport.

> **Ethics:** The moral principles that govern a person's behaviour.
>
> **Nutritional supplement:** A product taken to boost a person's intake of a certain vitamin or mineral.

Table 1.4 **Reasons for and against the use of PEDs in sport**

For	Against
Creates a level playing field by allowing all performers to take PEDs if they so wish (because some elite athletes are 'getting away with it' while others aren't).	It is cheating and contradicts the true spirit of sport and fair play. It also sets a bad example to young people.
Protects the safety and health of performers if PEDs are more closely monitored. (There is often only a slight difference between what can legally be taken (e.g. as a **nutritional supplement**) and what cannot.)	Even if monitored, there are many long-term health risks of using PEDs.
Protects the reputation of the sport for high standards of performance.	It will lead to a sport gaining a negative reputation.
Will lead to increased performance standards, making the sport more entertaining, which will in turn attract more spectators.	Media coverage as well as funding and spectator interest in a sport linked to acceptance of PEDs may be reduced.

Revision activity

Visit the UK Anti-Doping website (www.ukad.org.uk) to research their work as a national anti-doping organisation on fighting performance-enhancing drugs in sport via the sanctions and anti-doping rules they apply.

Exam tip

When answering extended questions, make sure you develop the points made and link them to relevant examples.

Typical mistake

Candidates often lose marks because they do not answer the question that is given. For example, in relation to a question focused on the impact of PEDs on the *career* of an athlete, do not give an answer that links to the impact on their health, as this is irrelevant and will gain no marks.

Now test yourself

TESTED

1 Identify **three** reasons why some sports performers may use performance-enhancing drugs. [3 marks]
2 Identify **three** reasons why sports performers should not use performance-enhancing drugs. [3 marks]
3 Describe the 'Whereabouts rule' used to test whether athletes have used performance-enhancing drugs. [2 marks]

LO3 Understand the importance of hosting major sporting events

The features of major sporting events

Major sporting events occur across the world on a **regular** basis. Some features of these events are described below.

Regularity/scheduling

Major sporting events require a lot of organisation, so they take place according to a set schedule at a certain time.

- **One-off** events are held once at a certain time or in a certain place (e.g. when a city hosts the football World Cup or the Olympics and Paralympics). Such an event may only occur once in a lifetime for many people as it may be the only time the event happens in the host city or country.

- Many major sporting events are held on a regular basis (e.g. they may occur on an **annual** basis). The UEFA Champions League Final is an annual event that is staged in different countries within Europe. Other examples of regular events include the British Open Golf Championship and the IAAF Diamond League athletics.

- In addition to annual sporting events, there are also **biennial** events such as the Ryder Cup in golf, as well as those that take place every four years (e.g. Olympics/Paralympics and World Cups in sports such as football and rugby). The host venue for these major events changes each time.

- Many major sporting events are **recurring**, meaning that they are repeated in the same place.

> **Regular**: Happens often at set intervals.
>
> **One-off**: An event that is held once in a certain place or at a certain time.
>
> **Annual**: Occurs every year.
>
> **Biennial**: Occurs every two years.
>
> **Recurring**: Periodically repeated in the same place.

Examples of regular and recurring sports events include:

- Formula 1 Grand Prix, such as the British Grand Prix at Silverstone
- Wimbledon Tennis Championships held annually at the All-England Tennis Club
- FA Cup Final held at Wembley Stadium
- London Marathon and Great North Run.

Figure 1.11 The Great North Run is a regular and recurring half-marathon held each September between Newcastle-upon-Tyne and South Shields in north-east England

International element

Lots of major sporting events have an international element, with performers competing from more than one country. This ensures a global audience and worldwide media coverage. International events include:

- the Olympic Games
- the Paralympic Games
- the FIFA World Cup
- the Rugby Union and Rugby League World Cup competitions
- the Netball World Cup
- the World Snooker Championships.

Investment in the event

Major sporting events require a very high level of **investment** in order to host them successfully. This is certainly the case now for the Olympic and Paralympic Games. London 2012 cost an estimated $15bn. The FIFA World Cup in 2018 cost the Russian Government $11.8bn for construction and preparation costs alone. The billions of dollars required now to bid for and then host major global sporting events means that only a few countries can now afford to be considered to host them.

Sponsors play a huge role in meeting the costs involved in hosting major sporting events to make them financially viable. For example, the Olympics has an initiative called **The Olympic Partners (TOP) programme** that provides valuable financial resources to pay for technology and staffing to support staging of the Games, as well as for the essential services required by athletes participating in the Games. The Games receive funding from corporate sponsors in exchange for the right to advertise, display their corporate logo and use the official Olympic rings on their products.

Investment: Money used to fund something (e.g. a sporting competition) in order to get something back in the future (i.e. profit or a successful outcome).

Sponsors: The act of supporting an event, activity, person or organisation via provision of finance, products or merchandise.

The Olympic Partners (TOP) programme: Provides exclusive marketing rights to the Summer, Winter and Youth Olympic Games to a few global companies, including Coca-Cola, Visa, Samsung and Toyota, in return for sponsorship. These companies provide major financial support to enable the Olympic Games to be staged.

Figure 1.12 Corporate sponsorship is a common feature of sporting events

Potential legacy of the event

The **legacy** of a major sporting event is very important and is often one of the reasons why cities and countries are keen to host major sporting events.

Sporting legacy

- Hosting a World Cup competition (e.g. the Cricket World Cup and the Netball World Cup in the UK in 2019) often leaves behind a positive legacy for a nation. This may take the form of increased public support for the home nation team and increased participation in the sport(s) played at the event.

- The London 2012 Olympics/Paralympics is viewed as having had a positive sporting legacy for the UK. The success of UK athletes in a variety of sports inspired others to become more physically active.

- This also resulted in improved sports facilities in areas around the UK, as well as sustained sporting success at elite level, as UK athletes continue to achieve high positions in Olympic and Paralympic medal tables.

> **Legacy:** The long-term benefits of hosting a major sporting event for the country, its people and its provision of sporting activities.

Social legacy

Hosting major international sporting events can help improve a nation socially by:

- improving the status or recognition of a country
- increasing its people's morale and feelings of national pride
- increasing friendships between nations and an understanding of other cultures.

Economic legacy

Hosting major sporting events can help improve the economy of a country in lots of ways, including:

- increased job creation
- increased investment in an area and its facilities
- new sports facilities that generate more income (e.g. via admission costs)
- commercial benefits, including increased external investment and sponsorship revenue
- increased tourism.

> **Exam tip**
>
> If a question relates to sporting legacies, make sure you link your points to the appropriate type of legacy – sporting, social or economic legacy.

> **Revision activity**
>
> Visit The Olympic Partner Programme website (www.olympic.org/partners) to learn more about the history of Olympic marketing and how this programme of Olympic sponsors supports the staging of the Games.

> **Typical mistake**
>
> Some candidates lose marks because they are not specific enough when giving an example of a global sporting event. For example, simply saying 'World Cup' or 'Formula 1' would be too vague to gain marks.

> **Now test yourself** TESTED ☐
>
> Give **one** example of each of the types of positive legacies (sporting, social and economic) that can result from hosting a major international sporting event. [3 marks]

The potential benefits and drawbacks of cities/countries hosting major sporting events

REVISED ☐

Hosting major sporting events can have both **benefits** and **drawbacks**.

Benefits

There are many **economic** advantages for a city or country that hosts a major sporting event:

- Increased investment in the development or improvement of transport systems to help cope with the large numbers of visitors and spectators expected to visit before, during and after the event.
- Increased investment in the local area leading to **regeneration**.

> **Benefits:** Positive outcomes.
>
> **Drawbacks:** Negative outcomes.
>
> **Economics:** The production, distribution and consumption of goods and services.
>
> **Regeneration:** Investment in facilities and delivery of services in disadvantaged areas and the empowerment of local communities in processes aimed at bringing an area 'back to life'.

- An increase in **direct** and **indirect tourism**.
- With effective planning of the event, increased spending can be generated by tourists and visitors as well as increased revenue from sponsors and other businesses investing in the area who would not otherwise have been attracted.
- There may be increased employment opportunities before and during the event, as well as, to a certain extent, after it.

Hosting a major sporting event may also bring sporting benefits:

- Increased popularity and/or participation in some sports as a result of people being inspired by their role models and the performance of elite athletes.
- Improvement of sports facilities or the building of new facilities for the sporting event, which benefit elite athletes and recreational performers alike after the event has finished.

Social benefits of a major sporting event include:

- Improved infrastructure (e.g. better road/railway networks, provision of **social housing** and new shopping centres) built as a result of hosting a major sporting event will benefit people who live in or visit the area where the events are staged.
- Successfully hosting a major sporting event will raise the status of a city/country – people get to see and hear about it via global media coverage. This **shop window effect** is a major benefit.
- Increased morale within a country is another positive outcome for hosts, particularly when the population of a country gets behind and celebrates the successes of its competing elite athletes.
- Increased morale may lead to increased integration and unity (community cohesion) within a country.

> **Direct tourism**: Visitors who come to the host city/country because they are attending a major sporting event.
>
> **Indirect tourism**: Visitors who come to the host city/country after an event, having been made aware of it as a result of global media coverage.
>
> **Social housing**: Rented housing providing affordable homes for people on low incomes.
>
> **Shop window effect**: Increased status of a city and country because it has been advertised to the world.

Drawbacks

There are also a number of drawbacks involved in hosting a major sporting event:

- The bidding process to host the event is very expensive and may be unsuccessful (e.g. the failed FA bid for the FIFA World Cup in 2018).
- The very high costs involved in hosting the event can be more than the revenue raised, leaving the host country in debt and possible financial difficulties (e.g. the costs of the 1976 Montreal Olympics are reported to have taken taxpayers 30 years to pay off).
- Sporting facilities may be under-used or even unused after the event if planning is not carefully thought through. Facility under-use is a negative legacy of a sporting event (e.g. 1992 Barcelona Olympic diving pool).
- The participation legacy may be limited – increased participation in a sport does not always result from hosting major sporting events.
- Hosting an event with a single focus sport (e.g. the Cricket World Cup) may only help to promote that sport and others may suffer as a consequence.
- If an event is disorganised or poorly run, it can have a negative impact on the status of a country.
- Public perception of an event can be negatively affected by the threat of terrorism or other controversy (e.g. political demonstrations in Brazil around the 2016 Rio Olympics).

- Hosting a major event may cause divisions within a country if the specific area hosting it is limited (e.g. 2012 London Olympics). The host city is seen as the only beneficiary and other areas of the country lose out or fail to see the benefits of being a host. This may lead to resentment at the use of public taxes to fund the event.
- The economic benefits/jobs created as a result of hosting a major sporting event may be only temporary or short term.

The links between potential benefits and drawbacks and legacy

REVISED

The benefits and drawbacks of hosting a major sporting event, together with the legacy each benefit should provide, are described below.

- **Development of facilities**: This can be very expensive, but it enables future generations to access high-quality facilities, increasing opportunities for the general population to take part in sport (sports development). This can benefit local communities as it enables people to come together to participate in sport (social development).
- **Infrastructure**: While the cost of improving transport infrastructure (e.g. airports, roads, railways) is very high, improved transport links will continue to benefit the population long after the event has finished (sports development/social development). In the twenty-first century, transport projects are built and run in a more environmentally friendly way (**environmental enhancement**).
- **Tourism**: Increased numbers of tourists may lead to over-crowding, noise, traffic congestion and perhaps pollution, but they increase the income of the host city/country by spending money (economic value). The shop window effect can help others to appreciate the cultural value of a city/country (cultural development).

> **Environmental enhancement**: Work which improves the environment and benefits conservation.

> **Exam tip**
>
> If the command word 'describe' is used in a question, make sure you provide enough detail in your answers to make your points clearly. Avoid one-word, bullet-point responses.

> **Revision activity**
>
> Visit www.theguardian.com/football/2010/dec/02/world-cup-2018-england-bid to explore a timeline of the failed FA bid to host the 2018 World Cup.
>
> Visit www.independent.co.uk/sport/olympics/after-the-party-what-happens-when-the-olympics-leave-town-901629.html to review the positive and negative effects on various host cities of the Olympic Games.

> **Typical mistake**
>
> Avoid giving only negative or only positive examples when asked to explain the effects of hosting a major international sporting event on a city/country.

Now test yourself

TESTED

1 Identify **two** sporting benefits to a country hosting a major sporting event. [2 marks]
2 Hosting a major sporting event can have both benefits and drawbacks. Outline **three** reasons why some countries choose to host major sporting events. [3 marks]

LO4 Know about the role of national governing bodies in sport

National governing bodies (NGBs) are independent bodies with responsibility for governing and managing their sport within a country. There is usually an NGB for every sport, recognised by the five Sports Councils (Sport England, Sport Scotland, Sport Wales, Sport Northern Ireland and UK Sport).

Examples of different NGBs and their focus sports include:

- Football Association (FA) (association football/soccer)
- Rugby Football Union (RFU)
- England Netball
- England Hockey
- England Basketball
- British Swimming (includes swimming and some water sports such as open water swimming, water polo, synchro swimming and diving).

NGBs fulfil a variety of different functions in relation to sport, as explained below.

> **National governing bodies (NGBs):** Independent, self-appointed organisations that govern their sports through the common consent of their sport.

Promotion

REVISED

A major role of an NGB is to promote their sport and increase its popularity. This can be achieved by promoting **participation** in the sport. An NGB is responsible for all sections of the community (i.e. all genders, religions, cultures, ages and ability levels).

Sometimes an NGB will decide to target its promotion to a particular section of the community. For example, the NGB could try to attract more women to take part by using strategies such as:

- taking part in wider sporting campaigns such as 'This Girl Can'
- providing equal access to sports facilities (e.g. via equal opportunities policies)
- providing taster sessions/women only sessions
- advertising female role models (and those from other less represented user groups)
- training more female sports coaches in their sport.

NGBs can also increase the popularity of a sport via participation schemes promoted in schools. This can be achieved by working with organisations such as the **Youth Sport Trust**.

> **Participation:** Taking part.
>
> **Youth Sport Trust:** A national children's charity which aims to use sport to improve the wellbeing of children and their prospects for the future.

Figure 1.13 'HSBC UK Ready Set Ride' is an initiative between an NGB (British Cycling) and the Youth Sport Trust that supports families and schools in helping children learn to ride a bike

The Youth Sport Trust works with NGBs to increase the popularity of various sports via participation schemes in schools, including:

- **HSBC UK Ready Set Ride**: HSBC UK, British Cycling and the Youth Sport Trust have collaborated to bring cycling to a new generation by empowering families and school communities to help children learn to ride a bike. The programme breaks the process of learning to ride into fun games across three stages.

- **FA Girls' Football School Partnerships**: The Youth Sport Trust and the Football Association have created a network of education-based partnerships with schools throughout England. The aim of these partnerships is to support the growth and development of girls' football.

Promotion of a sport by an NGB can also be achieved by increasing exposure in the media (e.g. TV, radio, newspaper, social media and internet) so that more people are aware of the sport. Examples of this include issuing regular press releases via social media about recent and upcoming events and **community engagement** projects where elite performers visit schools and sports clubs to talk about the sport.

> **Community engagement**: Developing a relationship with public bodies (e.g. local councils and schools) and community groups.

Development

REVISED

Another very important role of an NGB is to ensure performers are able to develop via clear, progressive **pathways**.

> **Pathways**: Structured routes for performers to progress through.

The Trampoline National Talent Development Programme is an example of a structured progression route:

- It aims to support young and talented gymnasts by providing them with training camps called High Performance Centres.

- These training camps provide specialised training designed to teach gymnasts the physical and mental skills needed for top-level success.

- The system has two tiers – Tier One for those who are performing well in competition and Tier Two for those who show the necessary talent to go on to become elite performers.

Development of performers in a sport can be achieved by NGBs in a number of different ways:

- Providing elite performer training and development – athletes may be selected for national performance squads (e.g. British Athletics prior to European, World and Olympic championships).
- Organising elite training camps (e.g. British Athletics elite training camp at altitude in Switzerland for middle- and long-distance runners).
- Awarding **central contracts** – in 2018, the England and Wales Cricket Board (ECB) awarded annual central contracts to 10 male Test players, 13 White Ball One Day International (ODI) or T20 male players and to 21 female players for 2019.
- Offering coaching awards via the development of an NGB coaching structure (e.g. following the UK Coaching Certificate (UKCC) structure from Levels 1–3).
- Training officials (see below).

> **Central contracts**: Also known as Elite Player Squad (EPS) agreements, these are used by the national governing body at the top level of a sport to contract a small group of players directly to their international teams for a specified period of time, such as one year.

Training officials

NGBs play a key role in the training and selection of officials to officiate at different levels of the sport they are responsible for. The Rugby Football Union (RFU) has a Young Officials Award as a starting point to encourage young people (aged 14–24) into officiating and provide a structure for them to progress through. Beyond introductory awards, there are further levels officials can work through to improve their understanding of the detailed laws of the sport and how to enforce them correctly during competitions.

Infrastructure

REVISED

NGBs are responsible for the infrastructure that is in place to support their particular sport. An NGB can help build the infrastructure of a sport in the following ways:

- **Creating and organising competitions and tournaments**: This can range from those aimed at grassroots and lower age ranges, through to senior and national level.
- **Deciding how rules are made, changed and administered**:
  An NGB must develop rules which correspond to rules that apply internationally (e.g. the Rugby Football Union develops rules in line with those of the World Rugby Executive Committee; the FA rules apply to every individual and team that plays football, regardless of level).
- **Developing and enforcing disciplinary procedures**: England Hockey provides detailed advice via its website of disciplinary procedures and ways in which players can appeal against any decisions made against them.
- **Organising a programme of drug testing**: All NGBs will have a policy relating to how they test athletes to ensure they do not use performance-enhancing drugs.
- **Providing a national directive and vision**: All NGBs must provide direction and vision for their sport in a country. The Lawn Tennis Association (LTA) aims to help people throughout the UK get involved in tennis.
- **Providing guidance, support and insurance to members**: A number of NGBs have an area of their website that only official members can access, which provides legal advice, guidelines and information on

how the member can access support and obtain insurance (e.g. links to insurance companies that the NGB has approved or policies that it recommends).

- **Assisting with facility development**: NGBs are an important source of expert advice on facility design and development, whether at international level or at grassroots sports clubs. NGBs are often seen as experts in providing valuable advice to grassroots sports clubs when they apply for funding to develop their facilities. Clubs that apply to Sport England's **Inspired Facilities** fund to develop their facilities will usually need the endorsement of their NGB in order to be successful.

> **Inspired Facilities**: A Sport England funding programme that helps local community and volunteer groups to improve and refurbish sports clubs or transform non-sporting venues into modern grassroots sport facilities.

Policies and initiatives

REVISED

NGBs develop and apply lots of policies and initiatives that set the direction and vision of their sport in that country. Policies will relate to areas such as customer care and complaints, equality and diversity, equal opportunities, social media guidelines, disability awareness, disability plan, transgender guidelines, **safeguarding** and whistle-blowing:

- **Anti-doping policies and guidance**: All NGBs will publish details on their website regarding procedures taken to prevent the use of banned performance-enhancing drugs. For example, the ECB's **anti-doping** policy clearly identifies a list of all substances that are permitted and those that are banned. The British Gymnastics website includes a section that provides detailed information on which drugs are banned, procedures for testing, advice on nutritional supplements and what is acceptable as a **Therapeutic Use Exemption (TUE)**.

- **Promoting etiquette and fair play**: All NGBs seek to promote high levels of etiquette, good sporting behaviour and fair play. The FA set up its 'Respect' campaign to improve the behaviour of coaches and parents by asking them to act as positive role models to those involved in playing the game so that football is played in a fun, safe and inclusive environment.

- **Community programmes**: NGBs involve themselves in community engagement programmes to encourage participation, fun and learning through sport (e.g. the Amateur Swimming Association (ASA) has developed the 'Swimfit' programme which enables members of the community to access an online coach to help them get fit and complete a series of swimming challenges). The FA has lots of community/grassroots projects such as those sponsored by fast-food chain McDonald's, which include 'Fun Football Festivals' and 'The FA SuperKicks'.

- **Information and guidance on safeguarding**: Safeguarding is an area NGBs have had to become increasingly aware of, following various high-profile cases of child abuse in sport (e.g. by football coaches at professional clubs such as Southampton and Crewe Alexandra). NGBs have a very important role to play in ensuring appropriate advice is given to ensure the safeguarding of children (e.g. via training modules as part of coaching awards). For example, England Handball recommends that any coach leading or coaching youth age groups in a solo capacity should have:

  ○ a valid **DBS** check

  ○ a minimum of Level 1 England Handball Coaching qualification

  ○ attended and completed a UK Coaching Safeguarding and Protecting Children workshop.

> **Safeguarding**: The actions taken to protect the welfare of children and vulnerable adults to ensure they are protected from harm.
>
> **Anti-doping**: Preventing the use of prohibited performance-enhancing drugs.
>
> **Therapeutic Use Exemption (TUE)**: The process of how an athlete can obtain official approval to use a prescribed prohibited substance or method for the treatment of a legitimate medical condition.
>
> **DBS**: The Disclosure and Barring Service is a public body which provides background checks (formerly CRB checks) of individuals' criminal records. DBS clearance is a requirement for working or volunteering with children and vulnerable adults, in order to prevent registered offenders having access to these vulnerable groups.

Funding

All NGBs and sports clubs require money (income) in order to operate.

Potential sources of income include:

- **lobbying** for funding from official bodies (e.g. from UK Sport for investment in elite performers)
- Sport England
- grants and government funding
- membership or national affiliation fees
- subscription or match fees
- the National Lottery
- media/TV rights and sponsorship/advertising
- donations
- merchandising sales
- admission charges/ticket sales
- NGB initiatives (e.g. **Football Foundation**).

> **Lobbying**: Presenting an argument that seeks to influence another's decision.
>
> **Football Foundation**: The UK's largest sports charity, channelling funding from the Premier League, the FA and the government into grassroots sport in England.

Funding distribution

Having generated income, NGBs must then decide how to spend (distribute) it. NGBs distribute their funds to a variety of sources, including:

- grants/funding awards to individual performers
- funding to help elite performers compete successfully in international sports events
- funding of grassroots schemes and initiatives in sports clubs
- education/schools
- community engagement
- funding sports venue/facility development
- initiatives focusing on increasing participation in under-represented groups in the community (e.g. ethnic minority groups or people with disabilities).

Table 1.5 shows how funding from an NGB could help a community sports club overcome a number of barriers to playing sport.

Table 1.5 How a community sports club could spend funding received from its NGB

Barrier	Strategy
Cost	Subsidise/offer discounted sessions
Lack of awareness	Increase publicity via investment in print media (e.g. leaflets/posters) and social media
Lack of access to facilities/specialist equipment/lack of transport	Fund free transport or invest in adapted transport; purchase specialist equipment
Lack of specialist/good quality facilities	Refurbish facilities or build better quality/specialist facilities
Lack of role models	Pay for use of positive role models to promote a sport (e.g. at a promotional/taster event)
Stereotypes	Highlight role models to challenge stereotypes
Lack of time	Invest in crèches/childcare provision; offer flexible programming of activities
Work restrictions	Finance work-based clubs or longer opening hours
Discrimination	Invest in anti-discrimination initiatives

Funding advice to members

NGB websites are a useful source of advice to members of that particular sport on how performers and club officials can apply for funding.

Support

NGBs provide many different types of support, via their website and telephone helpline:

- Technical advice in relation to equipment (e.g. safety equipment), venues and surfaces (e.g. information about appropriate artificial surfaces).
- Location and contact details for local clubs and how to get started or more involved in the sport (e.g. a directory organised into regions/counties with information such as directions to a club, age ranges catered for at a club, and when starter/taster events are held).

NGBs support the development of a sport at elite level by:

- providing national performance centres
- organising national performance squads, elite training camps and access to elite coaching
- training high-level coaches and officials
- providing funding support to elite level performers/squads/teams
- developing **Talent ID programmes**
- providing a clear progression pathway through to elite level sport.

> **Talent ID programmes:** A process of recognising current players and performers who have the potential to excel within their sport.

> **Exam tip**
>
> Answers to questions about NGBs typically score low marks, so it is worth revising this section in as much detail as possible so you can answer questions confidently.

> **Revision activity**
>
> Choose an NGB and do some online research into how it promotes and supports its particular sport. Areas to consider include how it promotes participation, funding and development of the sport and its infrastructure, as well as examples of policies and initiatives it is currently promoting.
>
> Some examples of NGBs are shown below, but there are many others you could choose.
>
> The FA – www.thefa.com
>
> England Netball – www.englandnetball.co.uk
>
> England Hockey – www.englandhockey.co.uk

> **Typical mistake**
>
> Do not use examples of grassroots organisations if a question asks you about the role of an NGB in developing sport at elite level. Make sure you link points on areas such as coaching and facilities to the higher levels.

> ## Now test yourself
>
>
> 1 Identify **three** sources of funding available to an NGB which it could use to finance its sport (e.g. development of new facilities). [3 marks]
> 2 Outline the role of an NGB in developing sport at elite level. [3 marks]

Unit R052 Developing sports skills

This is a compulsory coursework unit which is internally assessed (i.e. it will be marked within your school/college by your teacher).

The written assignment should take you about 10 hours to complete and is worth up to 60 marks.

The skills, knowledge and understanding you need are covered in four learning outcomes (LOs):
- LO1: Be able to use skills, techniques and tactics/strategies/compositional ideas as an individual performer in a sporting activity
- LO2: Be able to use skills, techniques and tactics/strategies/compositional ideas as a team performer in a sporting activity
- LO3: Be able to officiate in a sporting activity
- LO4: Be able to apply practice methods to support improvement in a sporting activity

This section of the Revision Notes summarises the required knowledge for each of the four learning outcomes, so you understand what evidence is required for each of the four tasks in your assignment.

Completing your assignment

- When you write up your evidence you will be supervised and you and your teacher will have to complete a declaration form confirming that the assignment is your own work.
- Your assignment can be typed or handwritten and you can include tables, graphs and spreadsheets where appropriate.
- If you include any material from a book or website this must be acknowledged and a reference provided. Any quoted material should be shown in quotation marks.
- Your completed assignment should have a cover sheet attached which includes your centre number, centre name, candidate name, candidate number, unit code and assignment title.
- Your marks should also be included for each of the assessment criteria.
- If you are submitting your work in a digital format this needs to be in a suitable file structure (see OCR website for more details – www.ocr. org.uk).

LO1 Use skills, techniques and tactics/strategies/compositional ideas as an individual performer

For Learning Outcome 1, you need to show understanding of the key components of performance for an individual performer in a sporting activity via your performance in that activity. To evidence this task, you can provide detailed witness statements from a teacher/coach that clearly state and comment on the skills/techniques/strategies/compositional ideas that you demonstrated in your chosen activity as an individual.

What theory do I need?

Performance of skills and techniques

- There are lots of individual sports which people can compete in on their own. Examples include athletics events (e.g. long jump, javelin), badminton, climbing, cycling, golf, squash and tennis.
- When performing as an individual in a sporting activity, you need to be aware of the key components of individual activity:
  - **Skills**: The learned combination of movements using muscles and joints so that a smooth and coordinated action is produced. For example, skills in tennis include serving, volleying, lobbing, smashing and so on.
  - **Techniques**: How individuals perform the same skill. For example, if you watch clips of ex-athletes competing, such as Paula Radcliffe (long distance runner) and Michael Johnson (200 m/400 m runner), you will see that, compared to the 'perfect model', they had very different but highly effective running techniques.
  - **Technical demands**: Different sports vary in their technical demands. For example, running is relatively low in its range of required techniques so is quite simple to do, but tennis has a variety of technical demands across a range of different skills.

Creativity

- Creativity involves the ability to create or react in a unique or unusual way. It involves using your own ideas to solve a problem.
- The ultimate aim of using creativity is to try and outwit your opponent(s) by doing the unexpected. For example, you might change from your usual 'expected serve' in table tennis to try and gain an advantage over your opponent.

Appropriate use of tactics/strategies/ compositional ideas

- **Tactics**: These are the plans an individual performer uses when playing against an opponent to try and exploit their weaknesses as well as personal strengths. For instance, using drop shots in tennis to an opponent who has a strong preference to remain on their baseline.
- **Strategies**: These are overall plans on how best to perform as an individual. For example, performing a front somersault as the last move in a 10-bounce routine in trampolining.
- **Composition**: This is generally linked to more artistic activities. It is the art of creating and arranging something. For instance, in an individual dance routine, composition involves the use of space and height, as well as the development of motifs in performance.

Figure 2.1 Synchronised swimming involves composition

Decision making during performance

- Individual sports require a range of decisions to be made during a competition.
- Decision making is based on what performers see, hear, touch and feel. It involves the performers selecting a suitable movement or skill from a range of possible responses that are stored in their memory.
- Regular practice is very important in perfecting skills which an individual can then use to help them make the correct choice of skill to execute in a particular situation.
- The speed of decision making required varies depending on the sport being played. Boxers require very quick decision making to instantly respond to an opponent's moves. Golfers can take time to decide the type of shot to play and club required to execute it, depending on where the ball is laying and the position of any hazards.

Ability to manage/maintain own performance

- Individual performers need to be able to continue during sporting competitions, even when things don't go as planned.
- When competing in a sporting activity, things often do not go perfectly. This can have an effect on a performer's mental state and the levels of confidence/arousal experienced.
- Arousal can affect both the physical and mental state of an individual performer. The physical effects include an increase in heart rate, muscle tension and sweating. Mental effects include experiencing negative emotions such as worry and nervousness. These affect the ability to focus on the key demands of the sporting contest the individual is involved in.
- Individual performers need to learn to control their arousal and maintain it at an appropriate level so that it doesn't impact negatively on their performance.

- Applied to Learning Outcome 1 in this unit, an example of when arousal becomes something you need to control is when your performance evidence is being filmed. Knowing you are being filmed, and that how well you perform will result in a good or bad mark being achieved for your performance, may cause an increase in arousal levels. It is therefore important to try and control your nerves, forget about the filming and do yourself justice when performing in your chosen individual activity.

  Here are some suggestions for controlling your performance nerves:
  - Picture yourself performing a skill perfectly before attempting it.
  - Think of a calming situation or a relaxing place you have previously visited and try to imagine the sounds and scenery.
  - Accept that it is perfectly natural that you will feel nervous before filming takes place.
  - Practise some deep breathing exercises beforehand that you can use during your performance.
  - Stay positive and focus on what is going well as opposed to dwelling on anything which does not quite go according to plan.

LO2 Use skills, techniques and tactics/strategies/compositional ideas as a team performer

For Learning Outcome 2, you need to show understanding of the key components of performance for a team performer in a sporting activity via your performance in that activity.

What theory do I need?

Performance of skills and techniques

REVISED

- Team sports are activities that involve two or more players working together towards a shared goal of winning.
- There are lots of team sports – examples include basketball, football, hockey, netball, rugby league, rugby union and volleyball.
- Most team sports require a range of skills and techniques to be performed in order to be successful. For example, in football you need to be able to move quickly in different directions, pass and control, head shoot, tackle and so on.
- In order to reach the highest mark band, it is important that you choose a team sport you are able to perform very well in (i.e. one in which you can show advanced application of skills and techniques):
  - In football, this would involve a range of passing (e.g. short and long, along the ground and in the air).
  - In cricket, this would involve evidence of consistent performance of a range of batting techniques (e.g. forward defence, cut shot, running between the wickets and so on).

Figure 2.2 Batting in cricket

Creativity

REVISED

- Showing creativity in a team sport involves using your own ideas to solve a problem by creating or reacting to a competitive situation in a unique or unusual way.
- In team sports, we tend to think of the creative player as the more skilful player, as they tend to do the unexpected or do something that others have not done before, when faced with a particular situation.
- Examples of being creative in a team sport:
  - Thinking of and using a new line-out move in rugby union.
  - In basketball, pretending to pass to a teammate, but then feinting/dummying (i.e. pretending to do a move to throw off an opponent) before starting to dribble and drive towards the basket.
  - A footballer or hockey player who flicks the ball over an opponent's head and then runs around them to collect their own flick.

Appropriate use of tactics/strategies/ compositional ideas

REVISED

- Using appropriate tactics/strategies/compositional ideas in a team sport can be based on decisions made by individual players, but also in consultation with teammates and/or a coach.
- A bowler playing cricket can decide themselves when to bowl a short-pitched delivery to rise up by the batter's head in order to unsettle them, particularly if they are showing signs of weakness against the short-pitched delivery.
- In rugby union, if a team has an effective set of forwards, the strategy of keeping the ball close to them rather than running the ball through the backs (where it is more in the open for the opposition to attack) could be seen as the best way to win.
- Composition is the art of creating and arranging something that could be a pre-planned set play. The short-corner routine in hockey is seen as a very important aspect of the game as it provides a good opportunity to score.

Decision making during performance

- Team sports require lots of instant decisions to be made during performance.
- In sports like basketball and hockey, for example, performers must decide who to pass to as they are running and dribbling to try and avoid losing possession.
- In order to access the highest mark band, you must show consistent, accurate decision making in the team sport you compete in.
- Decision making in a team sport is limited by how long it takes to decide what to do (i.e. reaction time) and usually needs to be as brief as possible so that correct actions can be initiated quickly. The strategies below can help improve your speed of decision making:
  - Predicting or knowing the opposition's preferred options when it comes to being in possession.
  - Spotting the signs or signals of what your opponent is likely to do next.
  - Using practice specific to your needs to improve your reaction time (e.g. practise deciding what to do in different situations, such as two against one as a defender in different parts of the pitch).
  - Trying to predict/anticipate an opponent's actions.

Awareness of role within/contribution to the team

- The majority of team sports will have specific roles to be performed within a team, so it is important to be aware of what contribution you need to make for the good of the team when playing each role.
- A left wingback in football is required to defend the left-hand side/touch line when not in possession of the ball, as well as providing width in attack when in possession.
- It is important to be adaptable during a match if circumstances change. For example, in rugby you may be required to act as a scrum half if the scrum half finds themselves at the bottom of a ruck and out of the game. In football, you may be required to act as a centre half if the usual centre half finds themselves out of position in the opposition penalty area following a corner.

LO3 Officiate in a sporting activity

In addition to performing effectively in an individual sport and a team sport, this unit requires you to be able to officiate in a sporting activity. You need to be able to position yourself effectively so that you can apply rules and regulations both accurately and consistently. You also need to ensure that all decisions are communicated verbally and non-verbally to performers and spectators alike while you officiate.

What theory do I need?

How to apply rules and regulations relevant to the activity

REVISED ☐

- In order to develop as an effective official in your chosen sporting activity, it is important to first learn the rules and regulations. These define how a team or individual can win and are designed to ensure fairness in a competition.
- Rules and regulations are often set and enforced by the national governing body (NGB) of a sport (e.g. England Netball).
- It is important to keep up to date with any rule changes so you can officiate correctly. Rule changes tend to occur at the start of a season.
- The regulations define the area in which the sport can be played and, in some sports, the surface on which the sport is played (e.g. clay courts vs grass courts in tennis).
- Some sports require more than one official to apply the rules and regulations as there are a variety of decisions to be made (e.g. rugby union, rugby league and football require a main on-field referee and assistant referees/touch judges, while tennis has an umpire and line judges/service line judges).
- Officials are responsible for ensuring that the correct number of players are involved/on the field of play at one time. This role is particularly important when substitutions are made, to ensure that one team does not gain an unfair advantage over another.
- Depending on the sport, officials may be required to perform a variety of roles, including:
  - keeping score
  - time keeping
  - ensuring facilities and equipment being used are safe and suitable for the sporting activity
  - ensuring performers are wearing appropriate protective equipment (e.g. gum shields and shin pads).

The importance of consistency

REVISED ☐

- When officiating it is very important to be consistent. This means always making the same decision in a given situation, regardless of what stage the game is at.
- When making judgements in a sporting competition, the best officials tend to be the ones who can see precisely what is happening in front of them and make the correct decisions based on this.
- Inconsistency by officials (e.g. booking a player for a late tackle but not another for the same offence) is often a major cause of frustration and negative behaviour by players.
- To develop consistency and make good decisions when officiating, you will need to gain as much experience as possible in this role. Watching other officials who do it well can help you to understand how they achieve consistency and may give you ideas that you can put into practice.

The importance of accuracy

- In order to officiate accurately, you need to know and understand all the rules of your sport. Studying rules to gain a detailed knowledge of them is important, but so is being able to apply them in practice accurately and correctly.
- The accuracy required when officiating involves knowing the rules and watching what is happening during play. Developing accuracy while watching what is going on requires experience and the ability to concentrate for long periods of time, so you can make decisions based on what you have seen rather than guess work.

Figure 2.3 In netball, the umpire should be able to understand and enforce the rules of the game

The use of signals

- Different sports use a variety of signals to indicate that a decision has been made by an official.
- Signals are used to indicate to players and spectators when an infringement or foul has occurred and why a player has been penalised. For instance, basketball referees have lots of different signals for things such as a player foul, travelling and so on.
- Sometimes when an infringement or foul has occurred, the official may allow play to continue and 'play advantage'. This is where it is important to see if the team that would have been awarded has an advantage or not in playing on. If they still have possession and are still on the attack it is good to signal 'play on' to all involved so they know what is happening.
- Arm signals are used in a variety of different sports to support the decisions an umpire/referee/line judge makes. To signal an advantage, a football referee will extend both arms in front of their body. Assistant referees in sports like rugby league, rugby union and football use flags to indicate decisions such as ball in and out of play.
- You should study in detail the signals used by officials in your chosen sporting activity by looking at the appropriate NGB website, and practise them, so you are familiar with them.

How to communicate decisions

REVISED ☐

- Clear communication of decisions is important to players, fellow officials, coaches and spectators alike. It can be achieved in lots of different ways but needs to be appropriate to the situation.
- Examples of effective communication of decisions:
  - Using simple/short answers in reply to questions from players.
  - Use of a whistle to clearly signify the start/finish of a game as well as any stoppages as and when required.
  - Use of a whistle to signify the seriousness of an offence (fault or other rule breaking), for example, a gentle blow to signify a lesser offence which has been noted and needs penalising, compared to a strong, loud blow to signify a more serious offence.
- In sports where there is limited contact with performers (e.g. golf, athletics), officiating is likely to be far more passive, with any instructions given verbally during breaks in play (e.g. confirmation of any decisions made).
- Treat everyone with courtesy and respect.
- Be firm but fair.

The importance of positioning

REVISED ☐

- In order to make correct decisions, it is important that officials are in the best position to make such decisions. Some sports have officials who are already in the right position (e.g. in volleyball the line judges sit in exactly the right position to see whether the ball is in or out). In athletics, a long jump take-off official sits in a prescribed position to see whether an athlete's foot has crossed the edge of the take-off board or not.
- Other sports require an official to get into the correct position to see the activity. For example, in football, rugby league and rugby union, the referee and assistant referees/touch judges can freely move around the pitch and along the touchlines to get into a good position to see what is happening during the match.
- Ways of achieving effective positioning are outlined below:
  - Develop the required fitness levels to keep up with play.
  - Get as close to the action as possible, so you can clearly see what is going on (but not so close that you interfere with the action and potentially miss out on things happening elsewhere).
  - Move efficiently to be in the right position at the right time.
  - As an assistant referee/touch judge, keep near the side lines to make judgements on the ball in or out of play.
  - As an assistant referee/touch judge, act as a second pair of eyes for the main official to provide expert assistance when reaching decisions such as off-sides, bad tackles and dissent (i.e. disagreeing with the referee or refusing to obey rulings).

LO4 Apply practice methods to support improvement in a sporting activity

As a sports performer, you need to be aware of areas you can improve on, what skills this applies to and what types of practice/performance improvement methods you could use to achieve this. You may also need to look at your levels of fitness or skilled performance.

You also need to demonstrate that you know how to measure improvement in the skills, techniques and strategies being worked on which you have identified as weaknesses in one of the activities undertaken for Learning Outcomes 1 or 2 of this unit.

What theory do I need?

How to identify areas of improvement in your performance in a sporting activity

REVISED

- **What are the key skills in the activity?** You should focus on improving the skills which are most relevant for effective performance in the activity you are doing.
- **Which key skills are strengths?** When analysing performance, you can probably perform some of the skills required reasonably well (your strengths), but you may struggle to execute some of the more difficult ones (your weaknesses). Occasional performance of a skill is not a strength because to be a skilled performer you need to perform skills consistently (e.g. successfully scoring penalty flicks or kicks in hockey and football respectively).
- **Which key skills are weaknesses?** Think about those skills which you cannot perform regularly and accurately – these are your weaknesses.

Types of skills

REVISED

All skills have to be learned. Once you can perform a skill consistently in a smooth and efficient manner, you will have mastered it and it will become a strength. Most sporting activities involve performing a variety of skills, all of which must be learned by starting with the basics and working up to more advanced levels of performance.

Examples of different skills are shown below.

Simple skill

- Limited decisions need to be made while doing the skill.
- Requires limited thought because it is easy to perform.
- Tends to be taught while the performer is a beginner.
- Learned relatively quickly.
- Transferable between different sports (e.g. jumping in netball, volleyball and football).
- Examples include running and jumping.

Complex skill

- Tends to be specific to a sport.
- Normally non-transferable between sports.
- Requires lots of decision making in order to be successfully completed.
- Taught after successfully learning and performing simple skills.
- Can take a long time to master.
- Team sports often require many complex skills to be learned and perfected.
- Examples include lay-up skills in basketball and reverse stick dribble in hockey.

Open skill

- Adaptable, so can be performed slightly differently each time it is attempted.
- The environment in which it is performed is unpredictable and frequently changes (e.g. position on the field of play; the positions of opponents and the positioning of teammates constantly change).
- Best practised in an open environment (i.e. one where the performer gets used to adjusting the skill because of the small differences in each situation they face).
- Examples include passing in football and chest passing in netball/basketball.

Closed skill

- Performed in a stable, predictable environment (i.e. one that is not affected by the people around you) where the player can repeat the actions consistently and there are fewer decisions to be made.
- Best performed and practised by repeating the same action time and time again.
- Examples include taking a free throw in basketball and shotput in athletics.

Types of practice

REVISED

If you want to improve your skill performance, it is important to practise. There are different types of practice that can be used to increase skill levels. The best type of practice to use will depend on the type of skill that needs to be practised.

Whole practice

- The whole skill is performed at once.
- Whole practice works very well with closed skills.
- Used when the skill performed is very fast and cannot easily be broken down into parts (e.g. a football goalkeeper practising repeatedly diving to their right to save balls kicked to their right).
- Good for simple skills which do not require much thought, as fewer demands are placed on the performer.
- Gives a performer a 'feel' for the whole skill and maintains the links between the different parts of the skill.
- Whole practice may not be appropriate for beginners as it can place unnecessary demands on a performer who cannot cope with all aspects of the skill at once.

Part practice

- The skill is broken down into parts which are practised separately.
- Useful for complicated skills (e.g. in athletics, the different phases of the triple jump can be practised separately).
- Good for skills which are part of a sequence.
- Can help maintain motivation as an individual successfully learns each 'part' of the skill in turn.
- Generally less tiring than whole practice as it provides opportunities for the performer to rest between each skill practice.

Variable practice

- The skill is practised in a range of different situations that could be experienced during a performance.
- Useful for open skills where the environment is unpredictable or constantly changing.
- Allows the performer to adapt their skills to changing environments, making it highly appropriate for open skills.
- Helps to prevent boredom as practices can be made more enjoyable, which increases performer motivation.
- It is, however, time consuming and can put unnecessary demands on performers if they are given too many things to focus on.

Fixed practice

- A specific skill or technique is repeatedly practised in the same way.
- Best undertaken with closed skills.
- Leads to a skill becoming ingrained and perfected by the performer.
- Can lead to boredom and fatigue as the performer does the same skill over and over again.

Methods to improve own performance

REVISED

There are a number of different methods that can be used to improve your own performance, as explained below.

Different types of practice

One way to improve your performance of a skill is to use a different type of practice, as this can give you a better idea of how the skill may be performed and may increase your motivation to train. For example, swimmers who spend many hours working on their skills in the pool may organise their overall training into separate sessions to include full stroke sessions, arm action only and leg action only, as well as strength and conditioning work using pulleys on land.

Altering context of performance

This involves changing the circumstances in which you are playing (e.g. by practising with other, more skilled/higher level performers in your sport). The idea behind this is to get you used to moving at a faster pace and to make decisions more quickly.

Use of tools to aid evaluation

When performing in a sport, you will do some things well and others not so well. Your aim is to try to do well as many things as possible and minimise the number of things you do less well. You will need to evaluate your performance and identify areas that need to be improved. Some performers can do this, but others find it difficult and rely on their teacher or coach to observe and evaluate their performance.

Tools that can be used include:
- video, DVD or digital technology to record a performance for analysis
- video analysis/motion recording to analyse via playback individual aspects of your technique with a specialist coach
- match analysis/motion recording to analyse both individual and overall team performances

- software programs that allow performers to compare their technique to see if they are using the correct angles or positioning their body correctly.

How to measure improvement in skills, techniques and strategies developed

Some common ways of measuring any improvement are as follows:
- **Completion of proficiency awards**: Many sports (e.g. swimming and gymnastics) have a range of different levels and awards that can be completed to show improvement has been made. Accessing the higher levels of an award is usually linked to improved ability to perform skills and techniques in that sport.
- **Keeping individual logs of performance**: This will hopefully show a pattern of improvement in relation to improved scores in matches played or times/distances being achieved, etc.
- **Keeping video diaries**: These tend to be easier for individual sports which take place in a relatively short time frame (e.g. gymnastics, trampolining, dance). Team sports with large numbers of players can be more difficult to film but can be used to show how you perform and improve over time if they focus on you and what happens immediately before and after your involvement in a game.
- **Peer observation**: Asking knowledgeable peers to observe your performance and provide feedback can help improve performance (e.g. a fellow student who has knowledge of the assessment criteria and a good understanding of the sport you are doing; someone you know who coaches the sport you are doing so understands the key skills and techniques it requires). A peer who has suitable technical understanding can identify mistakes and offer advice on how to correct them.
- **Monitoring competition results over time**: Records can help show progression. For example, you might learn that your team has recently beaten the team who defeated you the last time you played them.

Top tips for success for Unit R052

Learning Outcomes 1 and 2

To meet these two learning outcomes, it is important to demonstrate the key components of performance in a range of sporting activities. Some ways of providing this evidence are shown below:
- Provide detailed witness statements to meet the assessment criteria (to access the highest mark band).
- State and comment on the skills/techniques/strategies/compositional ideas that were demonstrated by you as an individual.
- The information/detail provided should clearly link with the assessment criteria and the wording contained in the specification for Unit R052 Developing sports skills.
- Make sure you include the sporting activity you have been assessed in your witness statement.
- While information on the level at which you represent your sport is useful (e.g. represent the school, district or county), it is not, on its own, sufficient to enable marks to be awarded.
- A list of permitted activities for Learning Outcomes 1 and 2 is available on the OCR website (www.ocr.org.uk).

Learning Outcome 3

To meet this learning outcome, you need to demonstrate effective officiating skills. Examples of ways of providing evidence of effective officiating skills:

- Provide detailed witness statements (to access the highest mark band).
- Provide details of a complex situation in which you were able to apply the rules and regulations which clearly apply to you as an individual.
- Provide handouts explaining the rules being applied.
- Note that while an officiating qualification award level achieved is useful (e.g. Young Officials Award in Rugby Union), this alone is not sufficient detail to enable marks to be awarded.

Learning Outcome 4

To meet this learning outcome, you need to demonstrate your ability to review your own performance.

- The emphasis here is on you to provide most of the evidence for this learning outcome.
- For access to the higher mark bands, you need to review your performance in detail and show an understanding of how to measure improvements in detail.
- It is important to use the terminology in the learning outcome when mentioning types of skills and practice and applying practice methods, especially when aiming for the higher mark bands.
- If you provide a separate section demonstrating your understanding of the application of practice methods, this should, wherever possible, relate to the sporting activity being reviewed and should be contained within the practice methods.

Figure 2.4 Reflecting on your performance is the key to future success

Examination guidance

About the exam

Unit R051 from the Cambridge National Level 1/2 in Sport Studies is about understanding contemporary issues in sport. This is a compulsory examined unit with a one-hour paper which is worth 60 marks.

You therefore have, at most, one minute per mark. You should also leave time to check your work.

All questions are contained in a booklet with lines to write your answers on. There are no optional questions so you must answer all the questions.

Question types

On your exam paper there will be a range of different question types such as true/false, multiple choice, completion of tables and extended answer questions. Questions 1 to 14 are a mixture of these questions and are worth from 1 to 6 marks.

At the end of the paper is question 15, which is an extended-response question worth 8 marks. It is assessed against a 'levels' mark scheme. These levels relate to the written quality of your answer. You should write in a structured way with accurate spelling, punctuation and grammar and use specialist terminology where you can to achieve the higher levels. Each level also includes a list of the required content you need to include to achieve that level.

Example of levels of response descriptions	
Level 3 (7–8 marks)	A comprehensive response: ● shows detailed knowledge and understanding ● makes many points, most of which are well developed ● is well structured and consistently uses appropriate terminology ● has few, if any, errors in grammar, punctuation and spelling.
Level 2 (4–6 marks)	A competent response: ● shows good knowledge and understanding ● makes some valid points, a few of which may be developed ● is reasonably well structured and uses some appropriate terminology ● has occasional errors in grammar, punctuation and spelling.
Level 1 (1–3 marks)	A basic response: ● shows limited knowledge and understanding ● makes some basic points which are rarely developed ● has limited coherence and structure, with little or no use of appropriate terminology ● has errors in grammar, punctuation and spelling that may be noticeable and intrusive.
0 = nil response or no response worthy of credit	

Command words

When sitting your exam, read each question carefully and identify exactly what is required. You might want to highlight or underline any key words that you think will help you understand what the question is asking for. If you do this, always highlight the command word as this will help you to plan the content of your answer.

Simple command words such as 'give' or 'identify' require less time and detail in your response than more complex command words like 'discuss' or 'justify'.

The following table shows the command words that could be used at the start of questions in your exam and explains what each word means you have to do.

Command word	What you have to do
Analyse	Separate information into components to identify and examine their characteristics
Comment	Look at the information and present an opinion that shows knowledge
Compare and contrast	Show the similarities and differences
Complete/fill in	Finish the task by adding in information where gaps have been left (e.g. in a table)
Define	State or describe the meaning of the term(s) in the question; give the meaning of something
Describe	Set out characteristics
Discuss	Present both sides of an argument or strengths and weaknesses
Evaluate	Make a judgement taking into account different factors/pros and cons and using available knowledge and experience
Explain	Describe, giving reasons and causes
Give	Supply information quickly to answer a question from recall
Identify	Recognise, list, name or prove something as being certain
Justify	Give good reasons for offering an opinion or reaching a conclusion
List	Provide a simple statement of knowledge/recall
Name	Provide appropriate word(s) or term(s)
Outline	Give a description setting out the main points/characteristics
State	Express an answer in clear/simple/precise terms
Suggest	Give possible alternatives; put forward an idea/plan

Key points to remember in the exam

- Make sure your answer is clear and concise – try not to waffle.
- Make sure you do not repeat information that is already given in the wording of the question.
- If a question wants you to apply your knowledge and understanding, you need to include examples.
- Look at how many parts there are to a question and make sure you answer all of them.
- Check how many marks your question is worth and match your points to the number of marks in the question. Mark allocations are provided in square brackets [ ] at the end of each question/part question.

- Try not to miss out any questions. You could pick up a mark with an educated guess!
- You don't have to answer the questions in order. If you don't know an answer straight away, don't spend time being stuck – move on to a question you can do and come back to the question later.
- Write clearly in the spaces provided in the answer booklet
- If you need more space to complete an answer, use the additional lined pages at the end of the answer booklet and clearly number the question(s) where additional answers have been written.
- Avoid writing anything you want to be marked in the margins and always indicate if you run out of space that your answer continues on additional paper (or at the end of the answer booklet if there is space).
- The examiner needs to be able to read your answer so keep your handwriting neat.
- The quality of written communication (QWC) is assessed via the final extended question, so focus on making this answer your best in terms of how you structure and write it.

Revising for your exam

There are lots of different ways to revise for your exam and you may find that some revision methods are better than others. Here are some ideas to help you:

- **Mind maps**: Read through a topic and then, without using your notes, put the key points into a mind map. Check to see if you have covered everything and, if not, add the missing knowledge to the mind map. You will then have a concise version of your topic notes. Your mind map doesn't have to contain only words – you could draw small images to help you if you like.

A mind map for values which can be promoted through sport could look like this:

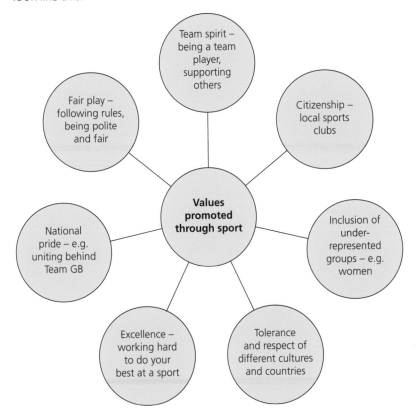

- **Exam questions**: As well as the practice questions later in this section, you can also visit the OCR website where there are lots of past papers and mark schemes (www.ocr.org.uk). You can use these to test your knowledge. You will also become familiar with the types of questions that could appear on your paper. Try to answer a whole paper in one hour without stopping, so that you get used to the amount of time you have available. This will prepare you for working under exam conditions.
- **Revision cards**: Simply read a topic and re-write your notes briefly onto small cards. Make sure you include all the main points. You may also wish to put notes on one side of the card and questions and answers on the other side.
- **Study buddy**: Revise with a friend and test one another.

Sample examination questions

Part A: Questions with correct answers

Question 1

Which of the following is not a user group experiencing limited access to sport? [1 mark]

a) Single parents

b) Ethnic minorities

c) People with disabilities

d) Employed/economically secure

> Correct answer:
> d) Employed/economically secure

Question 2

Link the sports initiative to the relevant sporting value(s) it promotes.

[3 marks]

FA Respect	Inclusion
This Girl Can	Fair play
Sport Relief	Citizenship/tolerance and respect

> Correct answers:
> FA Respect = Fair play
> This Girl Can = Inclusion
> Sport Relief = Citizenship/tolerance and respect

Part B: Questions with example answers

This section includes some sample exam questions and two sample answers – one that would receive high marks and one that would receive lower marks.

Question 3

State **three** possible barriers to participation in sport. [3 marks]

High mark answer

- A lack of time.
- A poor body image.
- Possible language/cultural barriers.

Assessment comment

This answer would gain three marks as all three answers are correct, relevant and specific.

Low mark answer

- Injury
- Lack of fitness to take part
- Age

Assessment comment

In this case the candidate has given two answers which overlap (injury and lack of fitness) and are verging on repetition, while the third answer is too vague.

Question 4

Identify **three** barriers which can prevent teenagers from participating regularly in physical activity and sport. [3 marks]

High mark answer

- Lack of time due to demands of school.
- Peer pressure (sport not seen as cool).
- Lack of money to pay for equipment.

Assessment comment

This answer would gain three marks. All three answers are clearly and succinctly made.

Low mark answer

- Time
- Money
- Lack of confidence

Question 5

A local community leisure centre decides to start up a new exercise class at 11 a.m., Monday to Friday.

Identify **two** user groups who are unlikely to be able to participate in this class. [2 marks]

High mark answer

Two user groups who would not be able to take part are:
- teenagers in education
- working singles/couples.

Assessment comment

This candidate would gain two marks. Two relevant points are made, correctly linking to the scenario provided.

Low mark answer

Two user groups who will not be able to take part are:
- school children in education
- retired people.

Assessment comment

This candidate would gain one mark, as one relevant answer is given (school children) but reference to retired people is irrelevant in the situation described. As this class is local and held during the day, they are likely to be able to attend.

Question 6

People with disabilities often find it harder to participate in sport than their non-disabled counterparts.

Outline **three** ways in which sport can be made more accessible for people with disabilities. [3 marks]

High mark answer

Sport can be made more accessible for people with disabilities by providing specialist transport such as a minibus with wheelchair access. Holding specialist sessions would also help, for example, disabled-only swimming sessions. It is also important to provide sporting activities which are tailored to people with disabilities such as Boccia.

Assessment comment

This candidate would gain three marks for their response to this question as three correct answers are outlined in detail. There is a clear understanding of the specific barriers to participation and how to tackle them.

Low mark answer

Lack of money and cost are barriers for people with disabilities, which means they participate less than people without disabilities. Lack of coaches is another barrier for them. To help increase participation for people with disabilities you could make physical assistance available to increase access to facilities (e.g. a hoist into a swimming pool).

Assessment comment

This answer would only gain one mark. One correct answer is outlined in enough detail (i.e. making it easier for people with disabilities to physically access sports facilities). However, the other two factors given do not relate specifically to this user group.

Question 7

Suggest **three** ways an emerging sport such as korfball can be made more popular.   [3 marks]

High mark answer

Korfball can be made more popular by holding more competitions, increasing the number of clubs to join and providing taster sessions for people to join in with.

Assessment comment

This answer would gain three marks for listing three different, appropriate ways to increase popularity of an emerging sport.

Low mark answer

- Provision of more facilities to do the sport.
- Media promotion.
- Advertising/promotion.

Assessment comment

This answer would gain two marks. It includes two ways of improving the popularity of an emerging sport, but the third point is a repetition of the second.

Question 8

Participation in recreational cycling tends to increase after major events such as the Tour de France and the Olympic Games, partly due to the increased media coverage it receives.

Apart from media coverage, describe **two** factors which impact the popularity of cycling in the UK.   [2 marks]

High mark answer

One factor which has impacted well on cycling as a sport is the continued success for British teams (e.g. Team Ineos) as well as individual athletes (e.g. Laura Kenny).

Another factor is that because cycling can be done quite easily on roads and cycle tracks, the facilities exist for many people to join in.

Assessment comment

This answer would gain two marks as the candidate has listed two relevant factors with suitable examples.

Low mark answer

TV, radio and newspapers all give lots of coverage to cycling at the Tour de France and Olympics. This creates lots of positive role models to aspire to and therefore encourages more cycling.

Assessment comment

This answer would gain one mark. The first factor given repeats the information from the question so earns nothing. However, the second point regarding role models is correct and so earns a mark.

Question 9

Explain different factors that affect the popularity of different sports in the UK. [8 marks]

High mark answer

One factor that affects participation in sport in the UK is media coverage. Some sports get lots of media coverage (e.g. football) while others get very little (e.g. badminton). This affects participation in a positive way if you get lots of coverage and negatively if you don't.

The previous success of sports performers/teams in a sport can impact on participation. The UK has had lots of successes in cycling (e.g. in the Olympics and Paralympics) which has encouraged more people to take up cycling, but a lack of success in sports like volleyball means that relatively few take up this sport. The environment/climate can make a sport more or less popular. In most of the UK, winter sports like skiing and snowboarding are difficult to do regularly, unless you have access to an artificial slope or indoor facility. In the UK, access to a sport like running (e.g. cross country/park running) is fine, due to the mixed type of weather/climate we have.

Finally, provision of things like facilities and activity sessions, etc., can affect participation, with lots of football/rugby pitches meaning these sports can be participated in on a regular basis compared to a relative lack of swimming pools which mean less people can swim.

Assessment comment

This answer would reach mark band 3 and gain seven marks. A very well-structured answer with few spelling, punctuation and grammar errors and a range of relevant content written in a detailed manner and developed very well with appropriate examples used to illustrate the points being made.

Low mark answer

Factors which affect the popularity of sport in the UK include role models such as Harry Kane, Steph Houghton and Chris Froome who can boost participation in sport. But if they don't exist they can put people off doing sport. Sometimes if a sport is ok to do it can encourage people to do it but if not you are put off it. Finally, if a sport has equal opportunities it can encourage participation but if not it can put people off.

This answer lies within mark band 1 and would gain two marks. It provides a very limited understanding of the factors impacting on participation. Three factors are given but very little attempt is made to develop them, apart from stating a few examples of role models. As this is an extended question, it is important to answer it in a well-structured way that uses appropriate terminology and has few errors in spelling, punctuation and grammar. The content should show knowledge (i.e. 4–5 points) of a range of different factors which impact on the popularity of sport, taken from the specification, before developing these points using examples as appropriate.

Question 10

The Davis Cup is a tennis competition which involves national teams of male professional tennis players playing a number of singles and doubles matches.

Identify **two** sporting values and describe how each is demonstrated by the professional tennis players competing in the Davis Cup.   [4 marks]

High mark answer

Sporting value: Team spirit

Description: The Davis Cup builds up team spirit as players support and work for each other.

Sporting value: Fair play

Description: The tennis players play to the rules (i.e. fairly).

Assessment comment

This answer would gain four marks for giving two performer-related sporting values and two correctly linked descriptions.

Low mark answer

Sporting value: National pride

Description: The country unites behind the team to support them.

Sporting value: Gamesmanship

Description: Players stretch the rules to make sure they win (e.g. take an injury time out).

Assessment comment

This answer would gain one mark for one performer-related sporting value but no correctly linked descriptions. The point about national pride links to the country, which is irrelevant as the question links to the performer. The gamesmanship point is not relevant as it is not a sporting value as defined by the specification.

In this type of linked exam question, marks for description can only be given if linked to the correct, clearly stated or named value in relation to players/performers.

Question 11

Identify **two** values associated with the Olympic and Paralympic Games.

[2 marks]

High mark answer

Value 1: Respect

Value 2: Friendship

Assessment comment

This answer would gain two marks for two correct Olympic values.

Low mark answer

Value 1: National pride

Value 2: Teamwork

Assessment comment

This answer would not gain any marks. This candidate has stated more general sporting values rather than those of the Olympics and Paralympics.

Question 12

Using examples, define the terms sportsmanship and gamesmanship.

[4 marks]

High mark answer

Sportsmanship involves adhering to the written rules of sport, but also the unwritten codes of conduct. An example of this is returning the ball to the opposition in football when they have kicked it out because of an injury to one of your team.

Gamesmanship is bending the rules and stretching them to their absolute limit in order to gain an advantage. An example of this is delaying a restart to a contest or running down the clock when winning via time wasting.

Assessment comment

This answer would gain four marks. The sporting values are correctly defined and linked directly to relevant sporting examples.

Low mark answer

Sportsmanship links to fair play and sticking to the written and unwritten rules of sport.

On the other hand, gamesmanship is becoming more evident in sport these days, where sports performers stretch the rules to their advantage in order to try and help them win.

Question 13

Identify **two** different ways of testing for the use of performance-enhancing drugs (PEDs) in athletics. [2 marks]

High mark answer

- Taking a urine sample.
- Taking a blood sample.

Assessment comment

This candidate has given two correct testing methods for PEDs to gain two marks.

Low mark answer

- Doing random tests to catch out the cheats.
- The whereabouts rule.

Assessment comment

This candidate would gain no marks as they have not identified any testing methods. The focus in this question is on ways of testing, not two strategies to try and eliminate PEDs in sport, as testing is the method already chosen.

Question 14

Discuss the reasons for and against taking illegal performance-enhancing drugs (PEDs) in sport. [8 marks]

High mark answer

There are many different reasons why elite performers take illegal performance-enhancing drugs (PEDs). Firstly, they see it as a way of improving their performance (e.g. taking EPO can help them improve their endurance and train longer/recover more quickly from training and competition).

Athletes often take illegal PEDs because they believe others are already doing it and they cannot compete if they don't (e.g. in 100 m sprinting there have been lots of positive tests over the years and suspicions that certain athletes are taking drugs illegally to improve their performance).

Secondly, athletes often feel the pressure to succeed in their sport and see illegal PEDs as the best way to do this. For example, athletes feel the expectation of their nation to perform well and give into the temptation to cheat in order to meet these demands and win awards.

However, there are also lots of reasons why athletes shouldn't take them.

One of the main reasons against drug use is that it is likely to cause long-term health issues (e.g. steroids are linked to heart attacks/increased aggression).

In addition to the negative impact on health, taking illegal PEDs is seen as immoral and against the true Olympic values/fair play principles on which sport should be played. For instance, when Ben Johnson won gold in the Montreal Olympics in the 100 m final, he was cheating his nation and fellow athletes.

Also, by taking PEDs, if you are caught it has lots of negative consequences to you as an elite athlete. Lance Armstrong lost his reputation as a clean athlete as well as his Tour de France titles, prize money and sponsorship.

Overall, there are lots of reasons why elite athletes may be tempted to take illegal PEDs but ultimately it is not worth it as the reasons against involve damage to you as a performer if you do take them.

Assessment comment

This candidate has produced a top-level answer worth seven marks, with a balanced, comprehensive response detailing a number of different knowledge points of reasons both for and against taking illegal PEDs. It is very well structured with no spelling, punctuation or grammar errors.

Low mark answer

I would argue against illegal performance enhancing drugs in sport (i.e. PEDs) for lots of different reasons.

Firstly, it is about morality and fair play. The true Olympic Value of fair play is lost when athletes cheat and take illegal PEDs in order to try and win, but do so by cheating. Secondly, it is about pressure. The pressure to win can be so great it can lead to taking illegal PEDS. Pressure can come from within yourself as you are not making the progress you would like or need to in order to compete at the top level. It might come from your coach who puts pressure on you to take PEDs in order to make progress and increase your chances of winning.

Third and finally, it is about the negative effects when you get caught. Athletes who test positive are often banned for a long time from their sport meaning they can no longer compete or earn a living from their sport. They have to give back any medals they have won as well as any money they have earnt as a result of winning unfairly.

Assessment comment

This answer lies within mark band 2 and would gain four marks. Only one side of the argument mentioned in the question is addressed, as this response focuses purely on reasons against taking illegal PEDs; there is no evidence in the answer of an understanding of reasons in favour. In terms of language, it is well written, but ultimately lacks balance in relation to reasons for and against taking PEDs.

Question 15

Give one example of each of the following positive legacies which could result to a country/city from hosting a major international sporting event.

[3 marks]

Social legacy: ....

Economic legacy: ....

Sporting legacy: ....

High mark answer

Social legacy: Improved understanding of different cultures.

Economic legacy: More jobs are created.

Sporting legacy: Increased participation.

Assessment comment

This candidate would gain three marks for three correct answers which demonstrate an understanding of each type of legacy that may result from hosting a major sporting event.

Low mark answer

Social legacy: Increased participation.

Economic legacy: Increased tourism.

Sporting legacy: Improved morale.

Assessment comment

This candidate would gain one mark for one correct answer stated as a form of economic legacy. Two out of three answers are unfortunately stated in relation to a different type of legacy. Candidates should be careful not to mix up the different categories, i.e. to list 'participation' as a social legacy and 'improved morale' as a sporting legacy, as shown in this candidate's answer.

Question 16

Describe **three** potential negative impacts to a host city as a result of staging an international sporting event.

[3 marks]

High mark answer

A host city may see increased unemployment after the event as jobs created are only temporary. A host city may also be in debt after the event due to the high costs involved in bidding for and staging the event. A host city may get a negative image/reputation if bad things happen during the event (e.g. political demonstrations or violence).

Assessment comment

This candidate would gain three marks for identifying and describing three correct negative impacts of hosting a major event for a city.

Low mark answer

A country gets a bad reputation if the event is badly organised.

Tourism and visitors into the host city may decrease after an event so would only be a temporary thing.

The governing body suffers due to high costs involved in staging an event.

Assessment comment

This candidate would gain one mark for this answer. Only one potential negative impact is described that is linked to a host city. The references to a host country (rather than a city) and national governing body are irrelevant, so gain no marks.

Question 17

Many cities and countries bid to host major sporting events such as the Olympic Games or the FIFA World Cup.

Explain the possible economic benefits and drawbacks for a country before, during and after such events.   [8 marks]

High mark answer

Before events such as the Olympic Games, there are lots of economic benefits to a host country. Investment in sports facilities and transport infrastructure can help in the regeneration of an area (e.g. East London in 2012). Lots of jobs are created to build these facilities and infrastructure. Drawbacks before the Games can include the expense involved in bidding to be a host which may well not be successful. If you win, the cost of building sports facilities might be huge and funds might be diverted from other projects which then do not go ahead as a result of a lack of funding.

During the Olympics, benefits include increased tourism with economic benefits (e.g. retail and food sales increase) and more employment opportunities (e.g. in the hospitality sector), but drawbacks include the fact that many of the jobs created are only short term and there are increased security costs which need planning for.

Finally, after the Games, there are still economic benefits resulting from public use of sports facilities built for the Olympics (e.g. via admission costs). However, jobs created might be short term and not exist after the Games, so people become unemployed and have to look for jobs again.

Assessment comment

This answer would gain eight marks (mark band 3). A top mark band answer requires an explanation of economic benefits and drawbacks across all three aspects of the question set (i.e. before, during and after the Olympics). It also requires a clear demonstration of understanding of the points being made via use of appropriate and correctly spelt terminology. This answer fulfils these criteria. It is also well structured and consistently uses appropriate terminology. Few, if any, errors in spelling, punctuation and grammar are evident.

A benefit is:
- Job creation to build facilities/grounds before the event as well as running the Games.

A drawback is:
- Jobs created are only short term and people are unemployed again when the Olympics ends.

Assessment comment

This would gain two marks, namely for providing one economic benefit and one drawback in a bullet-point list rather than continuous prose, with little or no use of appropriate terminology evident.

Question 18

Identify **two** ways in which national governing bodies (NGBs) such as England Netball are involved in developing their sport, giving an example for each.   [4 marks]

High mark answer

They organise elite training (e.g. through national netball performance squads).

They train officials (e.g. training and selecting netball umpires) to officiate at school/club level up to elite/super league level.

Assessment comment

The candidate would gain four marks for this response. Two correct points are made regarding NGB involvement in a sport's development, both of which are directly linked to two correct examples.

Low mark answer

NGBs are there to develop coaching awards in their sport.

NGBs are there to organise training of elite athletes.

Assessment comment

This answer would gain two marks. Two ways NGBs help to develop their sport are made for two marks, but no examples are provided.

Question 19

National governing bodies provide funding for sports clubs to help them overcome barriers to participation.

Complete the table below to illustrate one method they could use to overcome each barrier stated. [4 marks]

Barrier	Method to overcome this barrier
Cost	
Lack of awareness	
Lack of access to facilities	
Lack of time	

High mark answer

Barrier	Method to overcome this barrier
Cost	Fund discounted sessions
Lack of awareness	Invest in publicity via print media (e.g. leaflets/posters) and social media
Lack of access to facilities	Invest in private free/adapted transport
Lack of time	Invest in crèche/childcare provision

Assessment comment

This candidate would gain four marks. Four suitable suggestions are made of how funding can be spent to overcome each of the barriers listed.

Low mark answer

Barrier	Method to overcome this barrier
Cost	Subsidise sessions on offer at clubs
Lack of awareness	Make people more aware
Lack of access to facilities	Increase access
Lack of time	Use the money to increase the flexible programming of activities at a club

Assessment comment

Two marks would be awarded for this response. Two relevant suggestions are made for overcoming the barriers of cost and lack of time, but the responses given for the remaining barriers are not methods because they do not explain how money received could be spent to help overcome them.

Question 20

Identify **three** sources of funding available to an NGB which could be used to finance the sport (e.g. development of new facilities). [3 marks]

High mark answer

- Lottery funding.
- Income from media rights.
- Income from membership/national affiliation fees.

Assessment comment

This candidate would gain three marks. Three correct NGB funding sources are identified to earn full marks.

Low mark answer

- Sport England funding.
- Sponsorship revenue.
- Advertising revenue.

Assessment comment

This candidate would gain two marks. The first two funding sources are correct, but the third is a repeat of the second source, so would not gain any marks.

Now test yourself answers

LO1 Understand the issues which affect participation in sport

Different user groups who may participate in sport

1. a) Any two from:
   - retired people and people over 50
   - unemployed people
   - older teenagers who have left full-time education or have a more flexible timetable in post-16 education.

   b) Any two from:
   - school children
   - teenagers in full-time education
   - working singles and couples
   - non-working/stay-at-home parents of school age children.

2. d) People who are employed/economically secure

Ethnic minorities

1. Any three from:
   - lack of awareness or provision of an activity
   - lack of information about what is currently available
   - limited provision or lack of appealing activities which meet their needs as a working couple
   - fear of discrimination
   - possible language barriers
   - possible cultural norms
   - possible religious reasons.

2. Any three from:
   - use role models from minority ethnic backgrounds to encourage participation
   - advertising/targeted promotion of activities specifically to minority ethnic backgrounds
   - provide appropriate and appealing activity options for BAME people (e.g. programmes specifically designed to increase participation among minority ethnic people)
   - challenge discrimination via actively promoting opportunities for people with minority ethnic backgrounds to participate in sport via outreach and community-based sports projects
   - produce programming schedules, signs and advertising materials in different languages; provide translators and interpreters
   - challenge/overcome cultural and religious norms and religious observances (e.g. via flexible provision, including single sex/women-only sessions).

Retired people or people over the age of 50

1. Any three from:
   - decrease/subsidise the costs of participation in sport
   - lack of self-esteem can be overcome via senior-only sessions
   - access to medical advice prior to participation and continuing to monitor as appropriate via visits to health practitioners.

2. Any three from:
   - lack of income or disposable income
   - lack of mobility/fitness and an increased likelihood of health issues negatively impacting on participation (e.g. illness and pre-existing conditions such as osteoporosis)
   - lack of accessibility to sports facilities and equipment
   - lack of positive 50+/older role models to encourage participation
   - lack of awareness or information about what is currently available to retired and older persons
   - limited provision or lack of appealing activities which meet the specific needs of older people
   - possible lack of time
   - lack of self-esteem and confidence.

Families with young children

1 Families with young children
2 Any three from:
- lack of free time
- possible restrictions due to work commitments
- other family commitments and things she needs to do with her young children
- unaware of activities due to a lack of advertising
- no childcare provision or the cost of childcare
- too tired/lack of energy.

Single parents

Any three from:
- lack of activities which a child/children and single parent can join in with
- lack of time (e.g. due to taking children to school or to see their friends or attend activities)
- no appealing activities or programmed sessions to suit them
- limited income/disposable income and cost of participation (e.g. membership fees/transport costs)
- fewer role models/female role models for women who are single parents
- lack of awareness of activities or facilities
- lack of available and/or affordable childcare.

Children

1 Any three from:
- lack of family income/disposable income, making it less likely that parents/carers can afford the costs of participation (e.g. transport costs, lesson costs, cost of purchasing equipment for children as well as membership/entrance fees)
- child's lack of interest or motivation – other interests are more important than sport
- not enough appealing or good provision of activities (e.g. restricted times when children are able to participate); limited awareness of activities
- the requirement for supervision by an adult, parent or guardian; if unavailable, this limits participation
- access to sports centre/facility because of reliance on others for transport
- poor self-image/embarrassment/negative body image in children; lack of confidence; highly self-conscious when comparing sporting ability relative to other children

- lack of role models or parental encouragement
- limited school provision
- limited availability of coaches/coaching sessions to develop skills/techniques.

2 Any three from:
- taster sessions which give a flavour of an activity
- suitable programming (e.g. after-school clubs with fun activities)
- establish links between the school and local sports clubs
- run gender-specific sessions (e.g. girls only to help overcome issues linked to negative body image)
- display advertising featuring a variety of sports role models.

Teenagers

Any two from:
- decrease or subsidise the costs of participation or offer concessions
- promote schemes aimed at encouraging participation among teenagers (e.g. Sportivate)
- provide more activities to go to during school lunch break and after school.

People with disabilities

Any two from:
- make physical assistance available to increase access to facilities (e.g. availability of leisure assistant(s); provide a hoist into a swimming pool, offer accessible toilets)
- improve access to a building or around a facility (e.g. lifts to different floors, ramps and accessible parking available as close as possible to the entrance)
- provide a range of appealing activities and accessible group sports (e.g. boccia/goal ball/wheelchair basketball)
- provide specialist equipment (e.g. throwing frames in athletics; lightweight wheelchairs for use when speed of movement is required)
- provide specialist transport (e.g. a minibus with wheelchair access)
- provide specialist sessions (e.g. swimming pool sessions just for swimmers with disabilities)
- increase promotion of availability of events/sessions/equipment which improves access (e.g. include Braille on signs).

(Award one mark for a solution and a further mark for a relevant linked example.)

The factors which can impact upon the popularity of sport in the UK

Any three from:

- participation levels
- provision/availability
- spectatorship
- success of a team or individual
- acceptability
- environment and climate.

Current UK trends in the popularity of different sports

a) Any two from:

- relatively cheap (e.g. can swim for free in the sea)
- good availability of facilities/local pools
- easy to do alone
- viewed as a good lifelong sporting activity because it is non-weight bearing and helps to maintain health and fitness
- positive role models inspire participation (e.g. Adam Peaty).

b) Any two from:

- relatively expensive to participate (e.g. court hire and/or club membership fees)
- lack of accessible indoor courts (e.g. tennis)
- negative impact of climate and poor weather on ability to play
- lack of provision in school PE programmes.

The growth of new and emerging sports and activities in the UK

1. d) Ultimate frisbee
2. Any four from:

- futsal can be played indoors, which appeals in winter months; indoor facilities can be adapted quite easily to play it
- it is accessible to all levels/ages/abilities because it is easier to play than 11-a-side association football
- it is useful in developing skills for association football
- shorter matches mean it can be played in reduced timespans, which helps meet the lifestyle of certain participants (e.g. working singles)
- increased competitive opportunities available
- greater promotion of the sport.

LO2 Know about the role of sport in promoting values

The Olympic and Paralympic movement

1. a) True
   b) True
2. Any two from:

- respect
- excellence
- friendship
- courage
- determination
- inspiration
- equality.

Other initiatives and events which promote values through sport

1. Any one of the following:

Initiative	Value(s) promoted
Sport Relief	Citizenship; tolerance and respect
ECB's 'Chance to Shine' campaign	Team spirit; inclusion
FIFA's 'Football for Hope' campaign	Inclusion
Sport England's 'This Girl Can' campaign	Inclusion
The FA's 'Respect' campaign	Fair play; tolerance and respect
Kick It Out	Inclusion

2. Kick It Out = Inclusion
   Chance to Shine = Team spirit/inclusion
   Sport Relief = Citizenship/tolerance and respect

The importance of etiquette and sporting behaviour of both performers and spectators

1. d) Shaking hands with your opponents at the end of a football match.
2. Any two from:

- ensures fairness/a fair result is achieved
- promotes positive values (e.g. respect for others)

- helps to ensure the safety of players and their opponents
- sets a good example to young people and provides a positive role model to children and young people
- improves the reputation of the sport and encourages participation
- ensures an activity or game can be played effectively in a free flowing and enjoyable manner.

The use of performance-enhancing drugs in sport

1 Any three from:
   - pressure to win/succeed as an individual
   - pressure from the media/nation to win
   - pressure from coaches to try to increase chances of winning
   - gain money and fame as a result of success
   - improve performance (e.g. via improved fitness in terms of strength, stamina and power)
   - improve recovery time from training or injury
   - increase the ability to train longer and/or harder
   - mask pain
   - lose weight
   - level the playing field because of the belief that others are taking PEDs.

2 Any three from:
   - can lead to long-term ill health (both physical and mental) as well as addiction or an over-reliance on PEDs
   - negative consequences when found guilty (e.g. long-term bans)
   - financial penalties (e.g. loss of prize money; loss of sponsorship)
   - gives an unfair advantage over 'clean' athletes who have not taken PEDs
   - it is cheating and against the rules
   - it gives the sport a bad name (e.g. in cycling and athletics where there has been a mistrust of results)
   - it reflects badly on an individual and nation.

3 The Whereabouts rule requires that athletes must provide their location (outside of competition) for a 60-minute timeslot every day for a year. The athlete needs to be in an 'agreed place' so that they can be randomly tested there at any time. Three missed tests in a year will result in a sanction.

LO3 Understand the importance of hosting major sporting events

The features of major sporting events

Sporting legacy – any one from:
- increased participation/inspire people to participate
- improved/additional sporting facilities
- sustained sporting success at elite level.

Social legacy – any one from:
- improved status/recognition of a country
- increased morale/feeling of national pride
- increased understanding of other cultures.

Economic legacy – any one from:
- increased job creation
- increased investment in an area or facilities
- new sports facilities generating more income (e.g. via admission costs)
- commercial benefits/increased external investment/sponsorship revenue
- increased tourism.

The links between potential benefits and drawbacks and legacy

1 Any two from:
   - increased participation/popularity of participation in the sport increases
   - improved/additional sporting facilities to access sport after the event
   - sustained sporting success at elite level.

2 Any three from:
   - increased investment in the development/ improvement of the transport system to help cope with the increased numbers of visitors/ spectators expected to visit before, during and after the event; increased investment in the local area (i.e. regeneration)
   - increased tourism – direct tourism involves visitors visiting the host city/country as a result of attending the major sporting event, while indirect tourism is that which results from visitors visiting the host city/country after the event, having been made aware of it via global media coverage
   - with effective planning, hosting a major event can generate increased spending by tourists/ visitors as well as increased revenue from sponsors/businesses investing in the area who would not otherwise have been attracted to it

- increased employment opportunities/job creation before and during the event, as well as to a certain extent after it
- increased popularity/increased participation in some sports as a result of being inspired by the performance of role models and elite athletes
- sports facilities will be improved, or new facilities will be built (which benefit elite athletes as well as recreational performers alike after the event has finished)
- improved infrastructure/social facilities (e.g. road/railway networks/social housing/ shopping centres) built as a result of hosting a major sporting event will benefit people who live in or visit the area where the events are staged
- successfully hosting a major sporting event will raise the status of a city/country as people get to see and hear about it via global media coverage (e.g. Brazil/Rio in 2016); the 'shop window effect' is a positive outcome for successful hosts of major global sporting events
- increased morale within a country is another positive outcome for hosts, particularly when the population of a country gets behind and celebrates the successes of the country's elite athletes; increased integration/unity within a country (i.e. community cohesion).

LO4 Know about the role of national governing bodies in sport

What national governing bodies in sport do

1 Any three from:
   - government grants
   - lottery funding
   - Sport England funding
   - distribution of private donations
   - sponsorship/advertising revenues
   - income from media rights
   - membership/national affiliation fees.
2 Any three from:
   - providing national performance centres
   - organisation of national performance squads/ elite training camps/access to elite coaching
   - training of high-level coaches
   - training of high-level officials
   - providing funding support to elite level performers (e.g. squads/teams)
   - developing Talent ID schemes
   - providing a clear progression pathway through to elite level sport.

Glossary

100% me: UK Anti-Doping's education and information programme to help athletes retain an ethically fair, drug-free approach to sport.

4G pitches: Synthetic sport surface; also known as an all-weather pitch.

Anabolic steroids: Prescription-only medicines that are sometimes taken without medical advice to increase muscle mass and improve athletic performance.

Annual: Occurs every year.

Anti-doping: Preventing the use of prohibited performance-enhancing drugs.

Benefits: Positive outcomes.

Biennial: Occurs every two years.

Boccia: A target sport, involving soft leather balls, that is played indoors by athletes who need high levels of support.

Central contracts: Also known as Elite Player Squad (EPS) agreements, these are used by the national governing body at the top level of a sport to contract a small group of players directly to their international teams for a specified period of time, such as one year.

Community engagement: Developing a relationship with public bodies (e.g. local councils and schools) and community groups.

Crèche facilities: A nursery where young children are cared for (e.g. during a working day or while their parent is participating in sport/physical activity at a leisure centre).

Cultural norms: The standards by which we live – the rules and expectations of society.

Culture: The rules, customs and beliefs of a particular group or society.

DBS: The Disclosure and Barring Service is a public body which provides background checks (formerly CRB checks) of individuals' criminal records. DBS clearance is a requirement for working or volunteering with children and vulnerable adults, in order to prevent registered offenders having access to these vulnerable groups.

Direct tourism: Visitors who come to the host city/country because they are attending a major sporting event.

Discrimination: The unjust treatment of different categories of people based on characteristics such as ethnicity, sex or disability.

Doorstep Sport: Sport club programme (set up by StreetGames) which supports disadvantaged young people to participate in sport.

Drawbacks: Negative outcomes.

Economically disadvantaged: Someone who does not have enough income to meet basic needs and qualifies for state-organised benefits.

Economics: The production, distribution and consumption of goods and services.

Environmental enhancement: Work which improves the environment and benefits conservation.

EPO (erythropoietin): A hormone naturally produced by the kidneys that can be produced artificially and injected to improve the performance of athletes such as cyclists.

Ethics: The moral principles that govern a person's behaviour.

Etiquette: The unwritten rules concerning player behaviour.

Family commitments: Parents' and care givers' responsibilities and willingness to try to meet the varied needs of their children and each other.

Football Foundation: The UK's largest sports charity, channelling funding from the Premier League, the FA and the government into grassroots sport in England.

Free Swimming Programme: A Sport England initiative (no longer offered on a nationwide basis) that was designed to increase participation in swimming in England, leading to improved health and economic benefits. The initiative was based around local authorities providing free swimming for children aged 16 and under and people over 60 years of age.

Futsal: A variation on association football (soccer) played on a hard court with a smaller/low bounce ball.

Gamesmanship: Bending the rules and stretching them to their absolute limit in order to gain an advantage.

Grassroots: The most basic level of an organisation (e.g. local non-league football clubs, as opposed to elite football clubs such as Arsenal or Barcelona FC).

HIIT: High Intensity Interval Training.

Indirect tourism: Visitors who come to the host city/country after an event, having been made aware of it as a result of global media coverage.

Infrastructure: The facilities and systems that serve a particular area of a country or city/town, such as roads, schools, public spaces and leisure facilities.

Inspired Facilities: A Sport England funding programme that helps local community and volunteer groups to improve and refurbish sports clubs or transform non-sporting venues into modern grassroots sport facilities.

Investment: Money used to fund something (e.g. a sporting competition) in order to get something back in the future (i.e. profit or a successful outcome).

Korfball: A ball sport with similarities to netball and basketball played by two teams of eight players (four male and four female), with the aim of throwing the ball into a net.

Legacy: The long-term benefits of hosting a major sporting event for the country, its people and its provision of sporting activities.

Lobbying: Presenting an argument that seeks to influence another's decision.

National governing bodies: Independent, self-appointed organisations that govern their sports through the common consent of their sport.

Nutritional supplement: A product taken to boost a person's intake of a certain vitamin or mineral.

One-off: An event that is held once in a certain place or at a certain time.

Participation: Taking part.

Pathways: Structured routes for performers to progress through.

Racism: Prejudice, discrimination or antagonism directed against someone of a different race or ethnicity based on the belief that one's own ethnic background is superior.

Recurring: Periodically repeated in the same place.

Regeneration: Investment in facilities and delivery of services in disadvantaged areas and the empowerment of local communities in processes aimed at bringing an area 'back to life'.

Regular: Happens often at set intervals.

Religious observances: Behaviour in relation to religious customs (e.g. some religious people may not practise sport on certain days of the week, such as Sunday).

Retired people: Individuals who have withdrawn from their active working life and are no longer employed in an occupation.

Role model: A person viewed by others as an example to be imitated.

Safeguarding: The actions taken to protect the welfare of children and vulnerable adults to ensure they are protected from harm.

School–club links: An agreement between a school and a community-based sports club to work together to meet the needs of young people.

Shop window effect: Increased status of a city and country because it has been advertised to the world.

Sky Sports: Main subscription-based sports channel provider in the UK.

Social housing: Rented housing providing affordable homes for people on low incomes.

Social media: Websites and computer programs that allow people to communicate and share information via the internet using a computer or mobile phone.

Spectator etiquette: The rules or guidelines for spectators at a sporting event.

Sponsors: The act of supporting an event, activity, person or organisation via provision of finance, products or merchandise.

Sportivate: A Sport England/National Lottery funded programme which ended in 2017, but which aimed to get more 11–25-year olds involved in sport and physical activity.

StreetGames: National sports charity that seeks to make sport more widely available for young people in disadvantaged areas.

Talent ID programmes: A process of recognising current players and performers who have the potential to excel within their sport.

Terrestrial TV stations: Free-to-air TV, such as BBC, ITV, Channel 4 and Channel 5 in the UK.

The Olympic Partners (TOP) programme: Provides exclusive marketing rights to the Summer, Winter and Youth Olympic Games to a few global companies, including Coca-Cola, Visa, Samsung and Toyota, in return for sponsorship. These companies provide major financial support to enable the Olympic Games to be staged.

Therapeutic Use Exemption (TUE): The process of how an athlete can obtain official approval to use a prescribed prohibited substance or method for the treatment of a legitimate medical condition.

UK Anti-Doping (UKAD): The national anti-doping organisation in the United Kingdom.

User groups: A group of people with the same interests who use a product (e.g. a fitness class at a sports centre).

Walking football: An adaptation of association football aimed at getting people aged over 50 involved in playing football. The rules have been adapted and include no running and only limited contact.

Working singles/couples: Young adults who have work commitments and no children.

World Anti-Doping Agency (WADA): A foundation initiated by the International Olympic Committee based in Canada to promote, coordinate and monitor the fight against drugs in sports.

World Anti-Doping Code: Published by the World Anti-Doping Agency (WADA), the Code aims to ensure that anti-doping policies, rules and regulations within sport organisations and public authorities are the same throughout the world.

Youth Sport Trust: A national children's charity which aims to use sport to improve the wellbeing of children and their prospects for the future.

Youth Sport Trust Athlete Mentors: A scheme that involves using some of Britain's most successful athletes to visit schools and inspire young people to get involved in sport.